Stuart London

Malpas Pearse

Picture sources: British Museum pp. 14, 26, 28, 84;
Radio Times Hulton Picture Library, cover, pp. 18,
19, 37, 48, 52, 53, 62, 67, 88, 104, 112, 118; London Museum p. 34. Photographs in centre section:
British Museum 8; A. F. Kersting 5; National Portrait Gallery 2(a) and (c); Radio Times Hulton
Picture Library 2(b) and 4; Michael Taylor 1,
3, 6, 7. Guildhall Museum slipcase illustration.

SBN 356 02566 7

Macdonald & Co. (Publishers) Ltd.

First published in 1969 by
Macdonald & Co. (Publishers) Ltd.
St. Giles House, 49 Poland St., London W.1

Reprinted 1969

Made and printed in Great Britain by
Purnell & Sons Ltd., Paulton, Somerset

Discovering London 5

Stuart London

Malpas Pearse

Macdonald : London

Contents

Places to visit and suggested walks are found at the end of each chapter.

Cover: the city rebuilt after the Great Fire, dominated by St. Paul's and punctuated by the spires of other Wren churches.

Slipcase illustration: Visscher's panorama of London, 1616.

Introduction

This is a gossipy history; London in the 17th century was full of anecdote. The biographers Aubrey, Fuller and Walton feed us incidental detail, 'unconsidered trifles', and these make the city more lively than a perusal of State papers ever could. In the 19th century Leigh Hunt's *The Town* provided a further collection of anecdotes. The gossip is the flesh of Stuart London, but the skeleton was the city itself, spreading out into the country, replacing battered medieval houses with geometrically designed brick ones, establishing terraces and squares as the pattern London would follow until the present day.

One of the vital points is that London was so small that it was easy to walk across it. The same characters crop up all over the place: Milton, Penn, Herbert of Cherbury, Elizabeth of Bohemia, Dryden, and, of course, Pepys and Evelyn. London was their village.

There is very little domestic architecture left from the 17th century, but we do have the City churches, St. Paul's and the Banqueting Hall of Whitehall Palace. Covent Garden has a little trace of the glorious Piazza which was the wonder of its time. Yet wandering about the streets, it is still possible to catch a flavour of the Stuart citizens, with long curls or perukes, fashionable cloaks and elegant swords, travelling to a meeting of the Royal Society, to the King's Playhouse in Drury Lane or to watch Charles II feed the ducks in St. James's Park.

The London Jamey saw

James I made London the plum which he would pull out of his pudding at the very end of his journey. He had been brought up in the shivering north, an unhappy, insecure man, set about by Puritans who threatened him with the memory of his ungodly mother whenever he appeared to stray from a straight and narrow path. The beauty of the Stuarts had skipped a generation in him. His large head and feeble body would have made him a butt for present-day cartoonists. But he was at last the king of England, and entered his kingdom regally, determined to maintain the triumphant position of Elizabeth, even if his character wasn't strong enough for the job.

London waited for him. It was emerging as a commercial centre as well as the home of a magnificent court. The London merchants had even dared to contest Elizabeth's dictatorship. They wouldn't be ruled by a man from Scotland—speaking in an accent they couldn't understand—with a family that could become as much an expense to the State as the family of a vagrant picked up in a gutter in Cheapside. While James I made his slow progress, knighting the local gentry as he came, Londoners went about their business as usual, and strangers from out of town swelled their numbers. It was over forty years since there had been a coronation; so the pedlars, the showmen, the country gentlemen, scholars and foreign nobles came into the city to spend or take money.

London wasn't a pretty city. It was ramshackle. The buildings had been erected hotch-potch by amateurs. There was no great architecture. Houses were built like the toy houses of children, and since land was expensive and air was cheap, they were enlarged on the first and second floors so that they overhung the narrow streets like sailing ships in port. The first-floor windows belonged to living rooms; here the lady of the house would sit and watch the traffic below. It was from the upstairs windows that rubbish was flung down to rot in the narrow channels dug through the centre of the road.

On the ground floors of these high, gabled houses the shops of merchants were open to the street. Some shopkeepers went further and erected stalls in front of their windows so that even sixty years later Samuel Pepys caught his sleeve against the merchandise when he drove past in a carriage.

But in 1603 there were few carriages. Although Elizabeth had used the first coach to open Parliament the new transport had not really become popular. Driving in a London street would have been perilous. The narrow lanes were already overcrowded with pedestrians, many of them selling cress or fruit or threads and pins, so that their heavy baskets swung out from their hips and heads and knocked the passers-by.

Carriers came into London by wagon, rumbling over old London Bridge, which rattled dangerously but never fell. Some hawkers had hand carts, which they pushed ahead of them into the crowds and here and there the great ones came, and as the century wore on they had swaying chairs, held up by footmen, who might slacken their hold in any sudden crush and pitch the grand lady into the gutter where she would lie with the refuse until they had space and strength to haul her out again.

The City was small. Fleet Street, Holborn, Cheapside were its shopping centres. The Londoners were curiously dependent on country people. There was no room to rear your own stock, and so the City people relied on outsiders to supply them with all their food: vegetables and meat or fish. During the century more and more food markets were to be established in London. There were nine major roads entering the City and the continual passage of carriers created a whole new industry—of lodging houses and 'ordinaries' which were early restaurants.

Population and Plague

The Palace was at Whitehall. There were other royal houses in the country near London: Henry VIII, always greedy for another house, took over Hampton Court and St. James's Palace. To the south of London there were Nonsuch, Greenwich and Richmond. If the new royal family wanted to escape the stench and the plague there were plenty of other summer houses to visit.

St. Paul's was one of the most popular meeting places in London. It was an immense building—a landmark to the whole city. Not that Londoners needed much of a landmark; their city was so small—bounded on one side by the river and on the other by green areas like Finsbury Fields and the marsh which was to become St. James's Park. There had been a statute in 1580 which prohibited the erection of new buildings within three miles of the gates of the city and which tried to curb the growth of the population by making subletting illegal. This attempted 'green belt' was really a chain put around the city to prevent the spread of plague.

The cost of living had risen alarmingly in the second

half of the 16th century but wages had been fixed so that there was appalling poverty. The dissolution of the monasteries by Henry VIII had resulted in crowds of itinerant poor scouring the countryside, seeking work where there was none, and friars added to the hordes of beggars. Foreigners came to London in great numbers. The new commercial centre needed their skills and they needed a Protestant refuge from the excesses of Catholic zeal on the continent. In 1583 there were 5141 foreigners in London. There were no Jews; they had been banished by Edward I in 1290. Cromwell allowed them to re-enter but they came in pathetically small numbers. The English were hostile to them and to all foreigners. Nearly a quarter of the immigrants lived in villages outside London. They couldn't compete with the guild members in the City. French hatters settled in Southwark; French silk-weavers had a colony in Shoreditch and Spitalfields; Dutch printers came to Clerkenwell and every ambassador had his retinue. In spite of the antagonism foreigners enjoyed visiting London. The English were almost a myth on the continent, separated more by their character than they would ever be by the channel. While Europe was ripped apart by wars, famine and pestilence, the English plodded on their pedestrian way, living well, enjoying noisy pastimes and profiting by shrewd business deals.

The plague was the only problem.

Plague was a problem everywhere, but the over-crowded Londoners were acutely conscious of it. There were plenty of culprits blamed when it broke out. Obviously foreigners were thought to bring it in. Alternatively the carriers from the country were suspected of bringing the plague with their fresh meat and vegetables, but the real culprits were overcrowding and lack of hygiene.

The first curse of James I's reign was the plague of 1603. It spread because the town was inundated by

9

visitors, waiting to see a coronation, and it was to accelerate a fashion which was to continue throughout the century—moving away. The villages of Hampstead and Highgate were favourite refugees for rich City families. In the summer, when the threat of plague was most serious, wives and children would move into the country. As these suburbs grew, they were to join with the city to produce the great metropolis of today. But in 1603 the hillside villages in the north were too far away for plague to spread to them swiftly.

The Buildings
One of the reasons for the plague lay in the festering walls of the houses. The great city over which foreigners enthused would look like a terrible slum to us, perhaps only comparable with the shanty towns built for cheap labour in our own day. The houses were small and built of wood. 'The scurviest things in the world,' said one observer, '... nothing but Wood and Plaister and nasty little windows with but one little Casement to open.'

The government appreciated the dangers of fire. A year after he arrived in England, James I decreed that all houses built in London were to be of stone and that the fronts of new buildings were to be suitable for the street. He tried to achieve further order in 1620, and his son Charles I also tried to ensure that houses should be of durable material with thick party walls. But the city of London was always stubborn when dealing with monarchs. The citizens continued to build their haphazard timber dwellings and only the plague and the Great Fire of 1666 were to bring them to their senses.

A Foreign View of Londoners
In 1599, four years before the vivid royal entourage entered the city, a young German traveller called Thomas Platter came to see London and left a careful

record of his visit. Platter thought it was a splendid city. His picture of London at the turn of the century is still one of the best we have. He imagined the mayor of London must have an income of £100,000 to live so magnificently. 'As soon as anyone is elected mayor he may demand a gift of some thousand pounds from the city, not more than £10,000 however.' In return he held open house for strangers. Platter was flattered that the mayor sent 'two men of distinction' to invite him to dine, although he had never met the mayor, Sir Stephen Soame, who was a grocer. Platter was received by the swordbearer and led into a handsome room where the men greeted him warmly and the women kissed him. He washed his hands in scented water and the mayor's son said grace.

The meal must have been daunting. There were two helpings of roasts and stews and two servers to carve and fetch and carry the plates. As well as the best beer there were wines from Greece, Spain, Italy, France and Germany. Conversation flagged. Platter spoke no English and although the mayor tried Latin, French and Spanish, he could not make himself understood in any of them. Finally he thanked Platter for the pleasure of his company and the young German was taken home—by this time it was evening.

Food

Londoners ate a great deal—too much, thought some foreigners—and mainly beef. The English expected four square meals a day. This habit was grievously hit by the poverty in the 16th century—but the poor tended to stay in the country. In the city they lived well.

Bakehouses were carefully organised. Each one had a seal and loaves were stamped with this badge. There were prescribed weights and fixed prices and a choice between brown and white bread. Figs, cherries, mulberries and strawberries were grown in London gardens.

Dairyfarmers kept their stock on farms surrounding the city. Some went even further. In 1612 a man in Westminster infuriated his neighbours by keeping eight cows in his kitchen. They complained to the authorities because of the dangers of storing hay in the bedroom, not the insanitary presence of the cows.

Hackney dairyfarmers were supposed to be the best— and could charge more for their products. In 1654 they would sell butter at 10d a pound when it was only 6d from other areas.

Milk was thin and weak, probably because the cows had poor pasturage. At the end of the century asses' milk was to become popular with the rich—at a price, 3s 6d for a quart.

Fish was popular and surprisingly fresh. Platter mentions great quantities of pike, which were fattened with smaller fish to prepare them for greedy Londoners. Fishmongers kept pike in a tank and would obligingly slit one open for a prospective customer, remove the guts and allow the customer to judge whether the fish were fat enough. If the customer gave a 'thumbs down' the fishmonger hastily replaced the guts, sewed up the slit and returned the pike to its tank. They maintained the pike recovered sufficiently to live for another week and could sometimes even survive for months. Platter felt that fasting from meat was retained for two days each week in order to maintain the fish trade, for England was firmly Protestant.

Beef was the most popular meat; it was also the most expensive. It was supplemented with great varieties of game as well as the more conventional meats. Ready-made meat pies could be bought in shops. Sweetmeats and desserts were popular, and the English were notable abroad for having blackened, rotten teeth.

Forks were introduced at about the same time as the Stuart kings, but only among the rich. The average man ate with his fingers and a knife.

'Restaurants'

There were always food vendors moving among the crowds and selling snacks—pie-sellers, hot drink vendors and orange-girls. Inns and taverns supplied food and women would visit them as well as men to drink sugared wine. The men would smoke in the alehouses, for although tobacco had only recently been introduced it quickly became popular. And while they drank and lit their pipes, one of them would play; for the English were considered very musical, and taverns and shops would keep lutes for the use of their customers.

In 1613 there were over 1000 alehouses and victualling-houses in the small area of London. A good dinner could be bought for 1d. Many were considered 'honest and reasonable' but some overcharged, and visitors were warned to choose them carefully. Southwark's main trade was tavern keeping. Its position on the south bank made it an overnight stop for travellers.

The London Streets

One very good reason for the poor conditions of the streets was the legal liability of every house owner for the piece of street before his house. Unrepaired, dirty and evil-smelling, London streets disturbed the most broad-minded visitor. They were coated with black mud which could be thrown at anybody who was momentarily unpopular. Since the river provided most transport at the beginning of the century, the roads had been neglected. The streets were thought to be well lit at night as the century wore on, but at the beginning it was still sensible to carry your own lantern, or have it carried before you by your servant.

The Watch were a guard who acted as an early police force. And like the early police force they were a continual butt for jokes and pranks; their weapons were usually outdated. However, London was considered com-

A bellman of 1616; he would call the time to the citizens and also act as a watchman.

paratively safe and a loud shout would bring these guards running to the rescue. Although the poor wandered as beggars, strict Poor Laws swiftly confined them to workhouses and attempts were made to provide work for them.

Bands of robbers were found in London, waiting hopefully for a well-heeled traveller to turn the corner; but they were a more common danger in the lonely marshes and outlying roads, which were easy beats for footpads and highwaymen. Petty pilfering was a more usual crime in the city, with the odd handkerchief or purse snatched while the owners were at the play or shopping. The city streets were more dangerous for the hazards they presented to the unwary pedestrian, who could easily stray into an open sewer or fall over a pile of refuse.

Householders were supposed to take their slops and rubbish to the gutter running down the centre of the street; but it was much easier just to tip it out of the window. Rainwater washed some of the refuse away but as the channels became clogged much of the dirt was immovable. A flood of filth would be diverted into the houses, so a board was often fixed across the bottom of the door.

Public latrines had been set up in the 14th century but they were not properly cleaned and the smells caused great complaint. Private lavatories were privies called 'the house of office' and they were situated in the cellar or in a backyard. The night soilmen would come round at night to remove the refuse but they would then empty it into the Fleet Ditch or into the Thames, so that it would create another nuisance elsewhere.

Streets were noisy. The traders all had their own cries —over thirty in all—which they bellowed continually, as well as ringing bells. The apprentices who stood in front of the shops encouraging trade would add to the caco-phony. James inveighed against the 'little devils', asking one of the Lord Mayors to attempt to make the shop boys correct their noisy and loud behaviour.

Shops were congregated in areas. The goldsmiths were in Cheapside, where their stalls caused great gawping. Booksellers had their shops round St. Paul's. Butchers, pastrycooks and wine shops had sprung up in great numbers as the city grew and it was estimated that every sixth house was an aleshop.

The streets were also thronged with continual proces-sions, meetings and celebrations, of which the Lord Mayor's Show was a notable annual event.

Busino, a Venetian visitor attached to his Embassy in London between 1617 and 1619, described a Lord Mayor's Show in great detail. It came by boat, with grand painted vessels dipping up the Thames while guns fired salutes from the shore. The streets were over-crowded and squibs and firecrackers added to the noise and excitement. The City Marshal with two footmen tried to clear a road through the throng. He was also attended by youths with masks and fencing swords. (Sometimes water was squirted at the crowd to make it disperse.) The procession was like a Mediterranean carnival with carts drawn by effigies of lions and camels. These were laden with sweets, which were thrown into the crowd.

The Water System

All the dirt had to be washed away. The conduits which stood in various parts of London were monuments to men who were commercially enterprising as well as public spirited.

It was an offence to pollute wells but they were still polluted. In a London without police, there were no qualms about infringing a small bye-law which might prohibit you tipping your smelly offal down the nearest hole in the ground. There was a stone reservoir at Tyburn and main conduits were linked by pipes emerging at the east and west of Cheapside, Fleet Street, Cornhill, Dowgate and the Stock Market.

A rich man could connect his house to the main conduit by 'quills' or narrow pipes. A property owner would demand a quill as rental if the conduit passed under his land.

By 1581 a Dutchman, Peter Morrice, had been given permission to build a waterwheel under the the first arch of London Bridge. The power created by this pumped the filthy water in the Thames into the city conduits, through wooden pipes. In 1584 Bevis Bulmer erected a similar wheel at Broken Bridge by St. Paul's.

In 1609 Sir Hugh Myddelton was given the right to bring water into London from Hertfordshire. He planned a system of tunnels to bring pure water through 38 miles of countryside, via Islington, to the New River Head. It took five years to build and it was the foundation of the Metropolitan Water Board. The shareholders of the Myddelton Scheme will be paid royalties on this early water system until the year 2082.

The New River Walk in Islington is the original pathway of the canal. The offices of the Metropolitan Water Board, opposite Finsbury Town Hall in Rosebery Avenue, are on the site of the New River Head.

The Theatres

During Elizabeth's reign the theatre had risen in esteem. By the time James came south to London, it was flourishing marvellously.

The tradition of fairground theatres, in which charade Punchinello characters played out their parts on the back of a wagon, had been replaced by real theatre buildings, and some inns had performances in their courtyards. The first known theatre building had been opened in 1575 and it was in Southwark. Thomas Coryat, who published his *News of England* in 1611, was amazed that the actors were dressed superbly. Many actors were protégés of great noblemen, who passed on their slashed doublets, carnation-coloured hose and fantastically embroidered robes when they had lost interest in them.

Theatrical performances were usually given during the day. The stage butted into the auditorium, which was an open-air yard with galleries round the side. Favoured friends or rich men sat on the stage.

Thomas Platter saw a play 'in the suburb of Bishopsgate' and said that two or three plays were presented in different London theatres at two in the afternoon. The 'groundlings' who stood in the main yard before the stage paid a penny for the privilege. A seat cost twopence but a cushioned seat was another penny. During the performance food and drink were handed round.

The auditorium of the Red Bull in 1672. The apron stage jutted out into the audience. Rich playgoers sat at the side or in boxes.

The Globe Theatre, Bankside, in 1616. The theatres on the South Bank evaded the regulations of the City Fathers.

The actor-managers who controlled the theatres had some eminence in their small world. Even a playwright like William Shakespeare was able to retire to a great house in Stratford at the turn of the century, and to live on the proceeds of his plays. He was also commissioned to write plays for court entertainers.

His partner, Richard Burbage (who died in 1619), was supposed to make £300 a year from his company and the upstart Edward Alleyn retired when he was forty and bought the manor of Dulwich for £10,000.

Actors had been recognised as craftsmen by a statute of 1597 and so the tradition that they were vagabonds and beggars was beginning to disappear. The theatre was a lodestone for men who had aspirations and personality but no money or education. It was classless, transcending the boundaries of workers, merchants and nobles.

The main criticism levelled against theatres was that they were plague pits. In 1573 the City had asked for their suppression. But they simply moved across the water. At time of plague they would be closed temporarily but the companies would open as soon as they were able to do so.

The actors were all male. Boys played women's parts until the reign of Charles II. Puritan London would never have accepted a woman on the stage. Besides, it was traditional for boys to play in skirts and wimples. Shakespeare confused the theme by allowing some of his heroines to dress as boys—which must have pleased the noisy, precocious eleven-year-old actors.

Bearbaiting and Cockfighting

When Londoners were not walking about amusing themselves by looking at the shops or the play, they would watch bearbaiting or cockfighting.

Bulls and bears were baited at Southwark in Paris

Garden and they were even introduced into court circles. James I presented an entertainment of bears and greyhounds fighting to amuse a Spanish visitor in 1604. The teeth of the bears were filed so that they fought with their paws only.

Industrious Thomas Platter, determined to miss nothing, watched a white bull toss dog after dog. As the hounds fell back they were caught on sticks so that they wouldn't break their backs. At Paris Garden five or six hundred people attended the baitings on special occasions and paid a halfpenny each to go in.

Platter also went to a cockpit where contests took place for nine months of the year. The other three months were needed to clear out the bloody feathers. It was designed like a theatre, with a round table in the centre of the floor surrounded by ledges from which the cocks were teased into battle. A good contest could last four or five hours, during which time great excitement would mount and large bets, sometimes thousands of crowns, would be laid.

The Fighters

There were also contests between fighters who used their fists. Not only did fights arise over trivial arguments, but occasionally contests would be arranged. These were not as popular as they would be two hundred years later, but they would still draw a crowd of cheering onlookers. Fighs between women occurred later in the century, and these were considered more entertaining.

Other Amusements

Londoners did more to amuse themselves than watch cockfights, steal purses, eat meal pies in the ordinaries and jeer during the plays. One of the greatest attractions was a public punishment. Executions were the most popular. Burning heretics at the stake was less common than in Tudor times, but hanging, drawing and quartering was the method of executing political prisoners—a miserable death in which the victim was disembowelled while still alive. Another form of execution was beheading, and James I made himself memorable for sending Sir Walter Raleigh to the block, although on that pleasant day when he entered London he had not foreseen this event—and he certainly would never have imagined that his own son Charles would be killed in this way.

Public floggings and brandings were common. Less terrible punishments were sentences to stand in the pillory or sit in the stocks. These could be added to grimmer cruelties such as cutting off ears or slitting noses.

One of the interesting aspects of the Jacobean and Elizabethan character is that amusements were classless. There was no social distinction between the man who watched a play by Shakespeare, or who listened to a consort of viols, and the man who gaped at a public execution.

Curiosity was the motive. All were avid to see and hear everything—to experience everything. New ideas, such as tobacco, were seized on swiftly. It was a city of change. The newly discovered countries were a source of profit and speculation. Londoners felt they were superior, they felt they had the use of the world. Their fashions changed rapidly. Their ideas altered as quickly.

They were intelligent, skilled, musical, boisterous, rude and fearful. Their city was filled with the threat of fire and plague. These twin dangers ran through London like tremors before a storm. In the tragedies of 1665 and 1666 their worst fears were to be realised and purged, and afterwards London would alter its appearance and its boundaries.

But the London James saw was still a little town of great arrogance, suspicious of kings, bounded by the court at Whitehall. The centre of politics had been the

Tower. This menacing building swallowed politicians in one bite and rarely regurgitated them. Westminster had been a puppet Parliament, which had only begun to show signs of independence in Elizabeth's reign.

James I, surrounded by his favourites, riding carefully on an easy horse, thought he had come into Paradise. He had come into a hornet's nest. London never really welcomed the Stuarts. The city was to emerge from their rule with its own independence and its own enlarging identity. James came through the gate from the north and saw the well-dressed citizens; the wooden walls of playhouses flying the flag of St. George; the malodorous streets filled with apprentices; the high houses crammed together like teeth in a mouth; the river filled with boats, spanned by a busy bottleneck bridge. He had arrived.

Around St. Paul's

There is nothing left of old St. Paul's except the street names surrounding it and an effigy in Wren's building. St. Paul's is one of the oldest parts of London. When the builders working for Wren began their excavations for the new cathedral they unearthed pieces of ivory and wood which had been used to fasten the shrouds of ancient Britons. The Romans had built a temple to Diana near the site.

In the early years of the 17th century, St. Paul's was not a pretty sight. It had grown up higgledy-piggledy like the city around it, with Gothic sections, heavy Italianate ornaments clamped on to the old building, and a strange truncated shape. It had a splendid vaulted ceiling and it was a stupendous size. According to some authorities, old St. Paul's was 690 feet long and 130 feet wide and once had a spire 520 feet high. This was burnt down in 1561 and never replaced. The present St. Paul's is 463 feet by 227½ feet and the dome is 365 feet.

There was no important domestic architecture in London, and no town planning. The Stuart attempts to make Londoners build in stone and with some regard to health and aesthetics were not well received.

In 1631 Charles I attempted to smarten the cathedral, and commissioned Inigo Jones to build a new west front in the Corinthian manner; the design was splendid on its own but appeared peculiar tacked onto the conglomeration of styles that formed St. Paul's.

When the rebuilding started, Inigo Jones pruned away at the old building unmercifully and cartloads of rubbish were taken away and dumped in Clerkenwell Fields, where curio hunters were to rummage for the next two hundred years, seeking the Italianate ornaments which had been thrown there. The old cathedral was nearer Ludgate Circus than the present building and at a slightly different angle, turned less towards the northeast.

St. Paul's was not a cathedral to Londoners. It was their main meeting place and promenade. The great central aisle was called St. Paul's Walk and up and down thronged a gossiping crowd, their conversation overwhelming the sermons that were being preached as they passed through the building. It has been called the Bond Street of the time. In 1609 Thomas Dekker wrote at length about St. Paul's in *The Gull's Handbook,* a satirical manual for young gallants. He warned them to beware where they loitered in St. Paul's, since the central pillars were covered with posters advertising servants, and an innocent young man who stood too close to these might be taken for a footman or a journeyman apprentice. It wasn't sensible to wear spurs in St. Paul's, not on religious grounds but because the choristers would be entitled to a fine called 'spur money' and they would cluster round him 'like so many white butterflies'.

St. Paul's Walk was the place to show off your new fashions, and tailors waited about hoping to measure

The west front of St. Paul's by Inigo Jones. This was the new façade commissioned by Charles I, which was mutilated by Parliamentary soldiers.

young men for new clothes. By mounting 200 steps to the roof, one could see London stretched out around the building; you could carve your name on the leads—a note for posterity, which was to prove very ephemeral since the roof melted away in the Great Fire. Round the north door of St. Paul's clustered the ballad sellers, with sheaves of broadsheets, the precursors of newspapers, which might tell of a political manoeuvre or a hectic story of strange imaginary wonders. News spread fast in St. Paul's. It was the centre for gossip and for loud inaccurate information. Businessmen did more work there than they could in the Exchange.

St. Paul's Cross

To the north of the cathedral was St. Paul's Cross. This was an open-air pulpit, sited where the original Folkemete had been in the 13th century. In any crisis or festival, Londoners would gather at the Cross for news. Queen Elizabeth visited the Cross to take part in a thanksgiving after the defeat of the Spanish Armada. Proclamations were read there and then nailed up so that scholars could read them out to the crowds. Here the dean preached. In the 1620s and until 1631, St. Paul's had a notable dean, Dr John Donne, who was much more than a clergyman. He had gained his office by the usual favours and intrigues of the time, but before he became a churchman, he was a lawyer and in his youth he had a reputation as a wit and a gay blade. He went voyaging on one of those Elizabethan adventures that smack more of piracy than exploration. He married a woman to whom he was passionately attached and he was probably the greatest poet in the early 17th century. Certainly his metaphysical poetry is appreciated today, perhaps more than in his lifetime. But Donne had his audience in his own day. The Jacobeans, sinister, thinking men, held London like a silent volcano. It erupted politically at the time of the Civil War. It erupted physically when the plague and the fire extinguished the city. But while they were silent, Londoners were passionate. Their God was a jealous, vengeful character. Their religion was tortuous. They liked Donne's sermons, which were full of arguments suspended from each other and woven together with the intricacy of lace. Dr Donne's sermons at St. Paul's gave new scope to rhetoric and transformed a religious monologue into poetry.

St. Paul's Cross had become a symbol of authority. It could easily become a symbol of free speech. It was demolished by order of Cromwell. The cathedral also suffered under Cromwell. The city declared completely for Parliament and all its resources went to war against

27

Old St. Paul's and St. Paul's Cross. This was the medieval cathedral, which had lost its spire. The Cross became an outdoor pulpit.

the king. After 1649 when Charles I was beheaded in his own palace before an immense crowd of Londoners, the citizens thought they would be able to use new freedoms and to develop the power of the city. But London was a threat to Parliament, just as it had been to the king. It had wealth, it was united. London had its own trained bands of soldiers, militia who drilled in Finsbury Fields—merchants who put armour over their sober coats on Sunday and then marched about the city trailing their pikes.

Cromwell stationed soldiers in St. Paul's. He had to break the authority of the building. Until the Civil War the Dean of St. Paul's and his 200 priests had some political power and the shabby, decrepit cathedral had some eminence as a central meeting place. The Parliamentary troops stabled 800 horses in the aisles of St. Paul's. They kept the citizens awake by playing ninepins at odd hours. They began to break up the cathedral.

28

In the earlier years of the century St. Paul's had enormous wealth. The plate was gold and jewelled. Every niche in the building had an altar filled with treasure. This disappeared as the soldiers took possession. There was no money to pay the troops. St. Paul's had scaffolding round it. It had been there on and off since Inigo Jones had installed the west front over 20 years before. The building sagged on this scaffolding, supported on the cross-beams until some major reconstruction work could be done. It was decided to pay the soldiers with the scaffolding. So the troops pulled it down and sold it. They dug pits inside the church so that the beams could be sawn across them. These pits began to undermine the foundations.

All relics of the dead king had to be removed. There was already a danger that he might be a martyr. So the west front was altered into a parade of shops with apartments above and as the façade was split, beams were driven into Inigo Jones's Corinthian pillars, which crumbled.

When Charles II returned to London, he genuinely wished to improve the city. He appointed a surveyor-general, Sir John Denham, and told him to do something with St. Paul's. The only reasonable action would have been demolition but that was, of course, impossible. Denham began a laborious patching job. On Wednesday, September 4, 1666, St. Paul's was almost annihilated. It was the best thing that could have happened to it. One relic remained, and that was an oddly moving one. Out of the rubble came an effigy of John Donne. It had been made by a great sculptor of the early Stuart period, Nicholas Stone, and it showed the poet wrapped in a shroud. It was made six months before his death and it had been a conceit to show him already wrapped for the coffin. This effigy was burnt and stained by the fire, but it was returned to the new building, where it now stands in the south choir aisle.

St. Paul's School

The school of St. Paul's had been founded in the previous century by Dean Colet. It had become renowned for performances of religious plays by the turn of the century. These were so entertaining that the school was listed among the playhouses. Good boy actors were always in short supply. As soon as they acquired the understanding to take arduous female parts their voices began to break and they had to be employed in masculine roles. When St. Paul's School was putting on a play talent scouts from the Bankside theatres would gather in the audience. They may have come from the Globe, which had been built across the river in 1598. It was burnt down in 1613. Shakespeare had acted there until he could afford to retire in 1612 and boys from the company would have had parts in *Hamlet* (1602); *Othello* (1604); *Macbeth* (1606) or *King Lear* (1606). All these plays had meaty parts for the actor-manager of the Globe, Richard Burbage. Both he and Shakespeare were probably involved in a playhouse that was nearer than the Globe, in Blackfriars.

Not all the boys of St. Paul's were stage-struck. As the century grew older, a Puritan element crept into the school. This was brought about by the influence of a master, Alexander Gill, who was stubbornly determined to oppose the monarchy before the general public had begun to revolt against it. Gill finally wrote a satire in which he referred to James I and the future Charles I as 'the old foole and the young one'. He was called to order. His father, who was also an eminent scholar, knelt before the king and asked for mercy.

James I could never resist a scholar. He was too prone to think of himself as academic. He forgave young Gill, who returned to teach at St. Paul's. Among the pupils whom he influenced with his outburst was John Milton. He was a prodigy—a pale, golden-haired boy who learned amazingly swiftly. Other pupils at St. Paul's during the century included Samuel Pepys and John Churchill, the future Duke of Marlborough.

Around the Cathedral

The precincts of St. Paul's stretched rather further than they do today. However, the green area behind the cathedral gives more idea of the environs of the original building that was demolished in the Great Fire. Behind the building was St. Paul's Cross, close to the end of Cannon Street, and between there and Paternoster Row stretched an array of odd houses and shops. In these worked printers and stationers. St. Paul's Churchyard was the centre of publishing and only the Great Fire ousted the booksellers from the area into Paternoster Row. There was also a building called London House or Bishop's House, which was used for formal receptions. It disappeared in the fire.

The area around St. Paul's was walled and the Churchyard was a grassy enclosure in theory, but since it was a general right of way, it was probably beaten earth and mud. The street to the north of St. Paul's, Paternoster Row, was 'taken up by silk mercers, silk men and lace men; and their shops were so often resorted to by the nobility and gentry in their coaches, that often the street was so stopped up, that there was no room for foot passengers'.

The fire dispersed the fashionable silk mercers. Their trade went elsewhere when the City became unfashionable as a living area. Into Paternoster Row came the booksellers, printers and stationers, evicted from St. Paul's Churchyard by the new regime. They stayed near Stationers' Hall which still stands in Stationers' Hall Court, Ludgate Hill. This building was originally Burgavenny House, a corruption of Abergavenny. In the 16th century the Stationers' Company bought the old building and erected a plain wooden hall which, not surprisingly, burnt down in the fire. Wren designed the new building, which was erected in 1670.

Until the Copy Right Act of 1911 every British publication had to be registered at the Stationers' Hall and in their first century the entries included the first folio of Shakespeare's plays in 1623 and Milton's *Paradise Lost* in 1667. The hall has a new east front, added in 1800. In 1680 a society was formed to honour St. Cecilia. As tributes to Catholic saints were hardly considered correct in the anti-Papist times of Charles II, the Society was probably looking ahead to the days of the Catholic James II. However, they did enjoy their musical evenings, when a piece of commissioned music was played before they sat down to dinner. In 1687 Purcell's 'Ode for St. Cecilia's Day' was played before them for the first time.

If you walk eastwards beyond St. Paul's you are plunged into the streets of 17th-century London. By St. Paul's Garden stood the Cordwainers' Hall, which was destroyed in 1941. A little north of it stands St. Augustine's; only the tower is left of this church rebuilt by Wren between 1680 and 1687. There is a modern block on the right in Cannon Street, called Gateway House. In the entrance is a stone, which was once part of the gateway to the city. Dowgate Hill joins Cannon Street. At number 8 is Skinners' Hall. The company has had a building here since 1295, but it has been altered several times. The old building was destroyed in 1666, and the façade is later than the building which replaced that lost in the fire. Inside is a staircase and courtroom which survive from the 17th-century hall. Farther along is Monument Station, and behind it is the Monument. This Doric column, 202 feet high, was designed by Sir Christopher Wren and Robert Hooke. It was built between 1671 and 1677 to commemorate the Great Fire, which started in Pudding Lane on September 2, 1666, supposedly 202 feet from the base of the column.

Parallel to Cannon Street is Cheapside. This was the centre of the Londoner's world until 1666. The city he knew was bounded by the Fleet Ditch on one side and the Tower on the other. It was the great commercial centre, which would lose its eminence as rich citizens left the centre of the town, seeking to escape the plague by living in the country. Already the shopkeepers must have noticed that shops were opening as far away as Piccadilly, although they might have felt that London could never expand too far westwards—the ground was marshy and the river made it damp and unhealthy.

Cheapside was packed with shops on each side. They did brisk trade. On great occasions the conduit would run wine. Usually it ran water which was enough to create a central point for citizens.

In 1912 the Cheapside Hoard (now in the London Museum) was discovered under the floor of a house in the street. It was a wooden box filled with jewellery amassed by a careful merchant, at the beginning of the 17th century. It included gimcrack bits and pieces, but also such elaborate jewellery as a watch set in an emerald. Some of the pieces are copies of classical cameos and intaglios, proving that city merchants had a taste for the antique and that Shakespeare may not have been unusual in his interest in ancient Rome and Greece.

The main streets of the city were to suffer terribly in the Great Fire, which swept away the medieval and 16th-century buildings. Early 17th-century London was in the style of the Elizabethan houses we can still see in Holborn. Top-heavy through scarcity of land, these buildings were of lathe and plaster or timber. Stone houses were built outside the city when rich merchants resolved to become country gentlemen. Many of the families that made their money at the beginning of the century became a new aristocracy a hundred years later, for in England nothing stood still and classes fluctuated. Some of the Catholic gentry had suffered under the Tudors and they were eager to sell land to the coming men from Cheapside and Poultry. And many men who bought land

Cheapside Cross in 1623 during a procession in honour of Queen Marie des Medicis. It shows what the street was like before the Great Fire.

began to build pleasant Jacobean country houses, forty miles away from the pestilence and danger of the city. Many of the City churches were altered at the beginning of the century, and then completely restored after the Great Fire.

The City Churches

St. Giles Cripplegate, off London Wall, was damaged in the Second World War but restored in 1951. In 1620 Oliver Cromwell was married there. When James I entered London the vicar was Lancelot Andrewes, one of the translators of the Bible, who was to be buried in the church. The great cartographer, John Speed was buried in St. Giles in 1629, and so was John Milton, who died in 1674.

There is a lane called St. Helen's Place, leading eastwards from Bishopsgate. The church of St. Helen is dedicated to the mother of Constantine, and it was part of a Benedictine nunnery in the 13th century. St. Helen's escaped the fire and the Blitz. It has a Jacobean pulpit and a Restoration sword-rest in the chancel.

St. Katherine Creechurch (or Christchurch) is off Leadenhall Street. Although the tower is Elizabethan, the church was rebuilt between 1628 and 1631. Puritanical Londoners must have liked the church, for the plaster ceiling bosses are decorated with the arms of the City Livery Companies, but they disliked the service of consecration, held by Archbishop Laud in 1631 and they quoted it as evidence against him at his trial. The organ of 1686 was made by Father John Smith who made the organ of St. Paul's. The font is decorated with the arms of Sir John Gayon who was Lord Mayor in 1646 and had the good fortune to escape from a lion in Arabia. On October 10, a 'Lion Sermon' is preached to commemorate this happy event.

St. Olave's Church, Hart Street, is behind Fenchurch Street Station. It was bombed in 1941, but the vestry of

1662 was not damaged. It had also escaped the Great Fire. This was the church of Samuel Pepys, who erected a memorial bust for his wife Elizabeth, who died in 1669. The pulpit is thought to be carved by Grinling Gibbons.

St. Clement's Eastcheap, in Clement's Lane (off King William Street), was rebuilt by Wren between 1683 and 1687. The carving is 17th century and it has a memorial to Thomas Fuller who wrote Fuller's *Worthies* and who died in 1661. Another church rebuilt by Wren (1681-82) is St. Mary Aldermary, the church at the junction of Queen Victoria Street, Cannon Street and Queen Street. Some of the Tudor walls remained after the fire and they were incorporated in the design, which is a strange one for Wren. A citizen donor, Henry Rogers, endowed money to rebuild the church in its original style. Milton's third wedding, to Elizabeth Minshell, took place in St. Mary's in 1663.

Inigo Jones, who did so much to alter the London of his day, is buried in a Wren church: St. Benet's, Blackfriars, in Upper Thames Street. Jones died in 1652, in a grim London, very different from his city of masques and court fashions, and in a period when little rebuilding was carried out. Wren rebuilt St. Benet's between 1677 and 1685. Nearby is the tower of St. Mary Somerset, another Wren church, demolished in 1871.

St. Michael Paternoster Royal is off Queen Street Place, leading from Upper Thames Street to Southwark Bridge. Another Wren church, built between 1672-77, it was bombed and recently restored. St. Stephen Walbrook, behind the Mansion House, is a remarkable Wren church with a dome and interior pillars; it was built from 1672 to 1677. St. Mary le Bow, in Cheapside, is one of Wren's most successful churches; built between 1670 and 1683, it has a campanile 221 feet high. In the churchyard area is a statue commemorating Captain John Smith who died in 1631 and who is buried in another City church, the Holy Sepulchre in Holborn. Smith was the sea captain who was

A panoramic view of the city after the fire. This projection shows St. Paul's as it would be on completion. Citizens rebuilt houses on their old plots, and thus halted plans for new urban layouts.

rescued by Pocahontas, the Red Indian princess, who married John Rolfe in 1613. She came back to the court of James I, where she was a great success, even before the days of the Noble Savage. On the outside of St. Mary le Bow, on the west, is a memorial tablet to John Milton, written by Dryden. Milton was born in nearby Bread Street.

St. Vedast's Church in Foster Lane, on the north of Cheapside, is another Wren church damaged in 1940, but now restored. It has interior carving by Grinling Gibbons.

Wren also restored St. Lawrence Jewry; part of the Guildhall; St. Peter's, Cornhill; St. Edmund the King in Lombard Street; St. Mary-at-Hill, in the street of the same name; St. Nicholas Cole Abbey and St. Andrew-by-the-Wardrobe in Queen Victoria Street; St. Margaret Pattens in Great Tower Street; St. Magnus the Martyr in Lower Thames Street; St. Dunstans-in-the-East in St. Dunstan's Hill; and St. Anne and St. Agnes in Gresham Street. The Great Fire destroyed 87 churches besides St. Paul's.

Westwards from St. Paul's to the Fleet

If you walk westwards from St. Paul's you travel downhill to Ludgate Circus. To your left is Blackfriars, and to the right the area stretching up to Smithfield Market. In the 17th century it stretched no further. London was like a village. Clerkenwell was fields, and across the river were more fields and a few theatres and suburban buildings. The only bridge to the south was London Bridge.

Before the 18th century there was a gate at Ludgate. It had been rebuilt on the site of another in 1586 and as the city spread westwards it was to take all the traffic to the new London, which was to spread through Covent Garden, the Strand and Leicester Square. The other centre was Westminster with the bustle of Whitehall and St. James's Palace But the area between still had enough room for large gardens, palatial houses for noblemen—

and a ghetto of thieves.

Ludgate itself was incorporated into a prison for debtors. The gatehouse and surrounding buildings ran along the south side of Ludgate Hill. The area behind, stretching to the river, was Blackfriars.

There were no friars in the 17th-century city. The dissolution of the monasteries had so far aided the city in that their destruction had provided more room for houseing. Blackfriars was still a strange, mixed neighbourhood. Across the way was Whitefriars, which was even more seedy.

Off Blackfriars Lane is Playhouse Yard, where a theatre performed the work of Ben Jonson, Beaumont and Fletcher, and Shakespeare. It was built in 1596 and it was described as a 'private theatre' lit by candles. This suggests that it was a snug small place, which opened in the winter or in the evenings. Shakespeare lived nearby and may have played there, for it was owned by one of the Burbage family. However, in the reign of James I, the younger Burbages pulled the theatre down, preferring to work on Bankside, away from the prying eyes and regulations of the City Fathers.

Number 12 Blackfriars Lane is the Apothecaries' Hall. It is partly a reminder of the building of 1670 (when it was rebuilt after the fire) and partly dating from 1756.

Until 1617 the Apothecaries' Company was part of the Grocers' Company. Throughout the 16th century the status of doctors rose as medicine became a profession. The men who could mend broken legs, let blood and apply leeches did not wish to be associated with the mountebanks and quacks who visited fairs to pull teeth and practise primitive magic. The company provided a seal of respectability. It is one of the City Livery Companies and it is still an examining body for medicine and surgery. Inside the hall is the original staircase and courtroom with 17th-century panelling, a bust of Gideon de Laure, who was the doctor of that dismal ailing queen,

Anne of Denmark, and sketches of her husband, James I, and her son, Charles I. Adjoining the new offices of *The Times* is Printing House Square. This is the old printing office of that newspaper, but its history is even older. In 1665 the King's Printing House was established in this tiny court to print the first official newspaper, *The London Gazette*.

Baynard's Castle was the gloomiest building in London. This fortified house at Blackfriars was on the edge of the Thames. In the middle ages it belonged to the Fitz-Walter family, who had used it as a fortress and a prison, suspending prisoners from posts in the Thames while the tide came in and out.

Since the 14th century it had belonged to the crown but royalty made poor use of it. It was too far from Whitehall to house visitors. It was a persistent threat to the city, since it was the only fortified house near the centre of London. When it was burnt in the fire there was no suggestion that it should be replaced. New Bridge Street runs from Blackfriars Bridge to Ludgate Circus, which had been the opening of the Fleet River. Once there were elegant Restoration and Georgian houses on each side, but these were demolished as the city grew. Bridewell Place recalls the old Bridewell Prison which stood on that site. It had once been a royal palace, but Edward VI had surrendered it to the Church. Since then it had been a house of correction for women, and in the 17th century it was a threat for vagrants, prostitutes and thieves.

Places To Visit

St. Paul's and its Neighbourhood

How to get there : By underground, by Central Line to St. Paul's Station.

By bus. 4A, 69, 11, 13, 15, 18, 141, stop near the cathedral. Nos. 7, 8, 22, 23, 25, stop in Cheapside. Nos. 4, 17, 45, 63, stop at Ludgate Circus.
By rail: Southern Region to Black-friars or Cannon Street.

Eastwards from St. Paul's, past St. Paul's Gardens, along Cannon Street. Note Bread Street, Milton's birth-place; the Wren churches: St. Mary Aldermary at the junction in Bow Lane to the left of Cannon Street; St. Benet's and St. Mary Somerset Tower in Upper Thames Street; and St. Mary le Bow on Cheapside. This charts the riverside route of the Great Fire. Cut east to see St. Michael Paternoster Royal in College Street off Queen Street. Continuing eastwards, note Skinners' Hall, Dowgate Hill. Cross King William Street; note this route from London Bridge was the only access to the city from the south. Look at the Monument in Fish Street Hill behind the Monument Station. From here you can see how the fire went. It didn't reach the end of Great Tower Street but it cut down to the river and Billingsgate Market.

Go north-west up King William Street, past St. Clement's Eastcheap in Clement's Lane. If you have enough energy go up to Bishopsgate, cutting through here to see St. Helen's in St. Helen's Place. You can cut through St. Mary Axe south again to see St. Katherine Creechurch off Leadenhall Street. Back again in a circle from Creechurch Lane through Fenchurch Street you will find Hart Street—a continuation of Crutched Friars behind Fenchurch Street Station where St. Olave's stands, parts of which are 17th century.

The Wren Churches

From King William Street you can explore other Wren church: in Great Tower Street, Abchurch Lane, Lombard Street, Lovat Lane, St. Stephen Walbrook, behind the Mansion House and St. Giles Cripplegate, off London Wall.

North from St. Paul's

Beyond the cathedral is the churchyard, with a memorial to St. Paul's Cross, the new area of Paternoster Row and the junction of Newgate Street and Cheapside, the Stuart shopping centre. Notice the new buildings of St. Paul's Choir School in New Change. Visit St. Vedast's in Foster Lane (north from Cheapside), St. Mary le Bow in Cheapside. Notice the halls of City Guilds in streets above Cheapside, mainly later than the 17th century but on the sites of older buildings.

Note that the whole area was burnt, as far as London Wall and Cripplegate to the north; the end of Great Tower Street to the east and the Temple to the west.

From Cheapside walk up Newgate Street to St. Sepulchre on Holborn Viaduct. Looking over the side of the Viaduct you can see the route of the Fleet River down Farringdon Road.

West from St. Paul's

Ludgate Hill leads to the old gateway to London; remember the Fleet Prison in Farringdon Street and the slum areas round the Fleet River. Walk down New Bridge Street towards the river. Bridewell would have been across the road on your right. The road would have been a filthy river and the roadside was wharves. Turn left into Blackfriars Lane off Queen Victoria Street; you will also find Printing House Square. Remember Baynard's Castle, approximately where Blackfriars Station stands. The water front from here to Billingsgate would have been Wren's proposed quay frontage for the Thames.

The Old City : Plague and Fire

In 1660 Londoners welcomed Charles II with relief. Only eleven years before they had watched his father die in Whitehall. They had been essentially Puritanical and anti-monarchy. Yet suddenly they were cheering wildly as the dark young man returned from exile.

But it wasn't so sudden. The atmosphere had built up gradually. During the Civil War London was enthusiastically for Parliament and it was probably the weight of the city's wealth and loyalty that swung the tide of war, even more than the invincible New Model Army under General Cromwell.

Londoners sent their treasures into a fund for Parliament. The Thames stayed open, so international trade continued. Even more important, the commerce and the free passage resulted in continuous contact with the outside world. Charles I's army held few ports; after the fall of Bristol the king was cut off from the continent and his followers were not merchants who would travel abroad. Ambassadors continued to come to London and to forge new links with Protector Cromwell.

The citizens turned out in arms when the Royalist Army came as close as Turnham Green. The city militia and trained bands were a joke to professional soldiers but the honest burgher trailing his pike to drill in Finsbury Fields had immense enthusiasm for one object—to keep the king from London. For the king symbolised the effeteness of court life, high-church services and ostentatious expenditure.

The Stuarts were always disliked in the city. James I was a figure of fun, yet gloomy with it, full of learned saws and sudden whims of inexplicable tyranny. Charles I was considered oppressive. His taxes were resented by the citizens. They had been suspicious too of his monkey-faced French queen who had no time for them and who believed her husband should be an absolute despot.

When Charles I's head was lopped off with such apparent ease, there had been stunned silence. This silence echoed round Europe. Momentarily England was anathema—a country filled with regicides. But the horror was only momentary. Commerce had to continue and Londoners continued to trade with continental merchants so inevitably their foreign contacts accepted Parliamentary rule too.

There were insurrections; the Levellers and Fifth Monarchists hardly affected the city, but the unnatural enforced sobriety did. St. Paul's was wrecked. Maypoles and playhouses were forbidden; there was an oppressive atmosphere in which levity or extravagance was absolutely restricted.

After ten years Londoners wished for relief. The court had been an institution to fight against and grumble about, but it had provided work and amusement for a whole section of the population that was now depressed. So they welcomed Charles II. A new spirit entered the town. Foreigners flocked into it. New trades began and old ones received new life. The city was spreading. The Strand, Westminster and Whitehall had always been populated. Aldwych and Covent Garden were fashionable in the time of Charles I, but the Restoration encouraged the growth of suburbs where people could live who were dependent on the court and city for their livelihood, but who couldn't afford to live in the old centre.

St. Giles, Tower Hamlets, Islington, Clerkenwell and Holborn increased in size. Stepney, Bow and Whitechapel were no longer villages. They joined together, although they would still look pastoral to present-day observers. Along the river, areas like Wapping, Deptford, Greenwich and Woolwich were becoming miniature industrial centres, concerned with shipbuilding and armaments.

Outside the confines of the walls London was still green. There were fields in the centre of the city. The large houses had large gardens. Market gardeners cultivated land south of the river in areas like Battersea; the river was still filled with boatloads of passengers; huntsmen still rode out in the morning to Soho or Leicester Fields.

Then in 1665 the threat of plague, which had always overshadowed London, became frighteningly powerful.

The Plague

In the previous year there were stories of plague in Holland. There were fears for London too. It began in the suburbs. St. Giles was the area around Tyburn Way (now Oxford Street) and Charing Cross Road. Poor people lived here, dependent on London for their work. They lived in ramshackle tenements where disease would spread quickly. The first recorded death, supposedly of a Frenchman, was in Drury Lane.

There were provisions for plague. There was a pest house where the sick would be taken, to isolate them from their neighbours and to ensure that they had medical care.

But the sweating sickness was a strange disease, which we now recognise as bubonic plague. A man could be dead of it within hours, without having time to appreciate that he was ill. The plague took its first victim in November 1664. The winter frosts seemed to abate it a little. It crept eastwards like a fog—down Holborn towards the old city. Each week the numbers went up—not alarmingly, but from four to six and from six to eight. In April, 25 died in one week. There was a surge of hysteria. But this was checked in May. The month was cool for the time of year, with fresh breezes; they seemed to blow the plague away.

In the last days of the month St. Giles was suddenly struck, with whole families dying together. The deaths were concealed, or called 'spotted fever'; nobody wanted to face the terrible reality of plague.

In June the City was paralysed by fear. Wealthy families moved out, shutting up their shops and houses. The City government acted rapidly, appreciating the dangers of the exodus. The Lord Mayor stated that everybody must have a certificate of health to leave London, and the Mansion House was blocked by queues as crowds gathered to collect their certificates.

Since few deaths were recorded in the next week or so certificates were given readily and coaches and wagons moved out of London, some carrying the germs of disease in bedding or clothes.

There were rumours of barriers which would be set up at the city gates and at the borough boundaries of outlying villages. There was a desperate attempt to escape before these were erected. The shops shut and even when they stayed open, customers were cautious in their purchases. After two people had been seized by sickness in the Shambles or meat market, there was an understandable hesitation in buying fresh meat and sometimes customers would snatch it off the hooks without letting the butcher handle it.

Posies had always been a remedy against the plague; even now judges carry them as a memento of the days when prisoners brought disease into the courtroom. As well as carrying flowers, Londoners now carried bottles of perfume and of vinegar to allay the odour of the plague.

By late summer Clerkenwell, Shoreditch, Bishopsgate, Moorgate, Whitechapel and Stepney had all been affected and so the illness crept into the City which now assumed an air of desertion. Prudent citizens laid in stores as if they were to be besieged and then shut their doors against the world. The rich could do this, and they could follow the harsh regulations laid down by the City council. But the poor had no money with which to lay in a stock of food. They couldn't afford to stop working; when work stopped, they would have starved if they hadn't travelled into the City to see what they could pick up from empty buildings.

What they did pick up was loot. The deserted houses were easily broken into when the Watch were busily occupied with plague victims. In stealing from the dead, the robbers carried the plague even farther.

The City authorities acted swiftly and with amazing foresight considering how ignorant they were of the causes of the disease. Immediately plague affected a family, it was reported to emergency wardens. The house was then virtually sealed up with its occupants inside and watchmen took shifts outside the door to make sure that nobody entered or left the house. The watch delivered food and medicine to the household. The dead were buried immediately; no bodies were to be seen in the City during the day, even when the plague was at its height.

When a plague case was reported a 'searcher' would visit the house to identify the illness. These were respectable women who would not handle food or do any work connected with the public apart from this gruesome task.

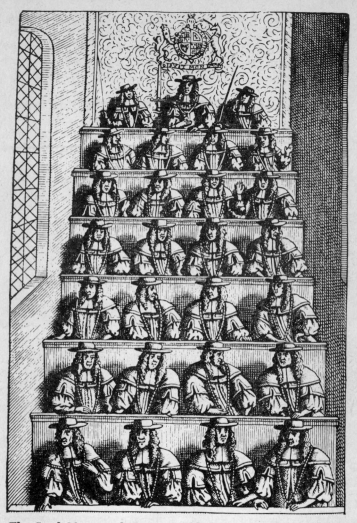

*The Lord Mayor and Court of Aldermen. The City authorities
stopped panic during the plague and issued certificates of health to
those leaving the city.*

Anybody who was involved with a plague case had to stay in quarantine for 28 days.

Doctors were appointed by the Lord Mayor, to visit the sick and to suggest remedies. Unfortunately there was no remedy except the isolation of cases. As many victims as possible were taken to pest houses although the existing pest houses were quickly filled and there was hardly room for the overwhelming numbers of sick.

Burials were made at night, in deep pits on the out-skirts of the city. There were no coffins, no mourners and no services. Every house visited by plague was marked with a foot-high red cross and the words 'Lord Have Mercy on Us'. This was less an invocation for aid than a signal to strangers that the house must not be approached.

The laystalls—or public dungheaps—were removed from the centre of the city. Streets were swept clean. Each householder was responsible for the area outside his door, but this regulation had not been adhered to; now it was enforced. Before every sixth house a bonfire was lit, supposedly to cleanse the air. At night plague carts collected the dead and carried them to burial. There were bitter complaints. Many householders easily evaded the rules. They often escaped from houses which had been isolated by changing the locks or going out through neighbours' gardens. The looting reached frightening proportions as the plague increased. The fear of the plague often caused more distress than the disease; negligible illnesses were thought to be signs of plague and so the sick would be crowded in with the plague victims. Some died of fear, thinking they had been in contact with the plague—and many committed suicide. The signs of the illness were vomiting, sweating, dizzi-ness and blotches on the skin, which broke out into abscesses in the groin and under the arm. These swell-ings heralded the last phase of the illness.

As G. M. Trevelyan points out in his *English Social*

History, it was not the numbers of the dead that appalled Londoners but the period in which it came; for it was 'in an age of greater civilization, comfort and security' when such perils were almost forgotten.

The plague affected the growth of London to the west. Inhabitants who could afford to leave the old city deserted it and even left Covent Garden and Drury Lane to travel beyond St. James's, hoping that the prevailing winds would drive the air of pestilence in the other direction.

By the summer of 1666 London was reorganising itself. The calamity had not been confined to the city. Too many people had carried the plague into the country. There are records of forty dead in a small town like Woburn and the odd farmhouse or village was decimated when infected food or clothing arrived from London. It took time to recover. There were stories of grass growing in the City streets. There was a feeling of gloom and Biblical despondency. In a superstitious age the plague had seemed a sign of calamity sent by heaven.

It was followed by a blessing in a terrible disguise.

The Great Fire

The summer was almost over and the plague had almost gone. Those who had left the city came back. The other general fear in London was fire. It was not unusual. Timber houses and thatched roofs would flare up suddenly in hot summers. Neighbours and the Watch would turn out and pull the roofs with hooks on poles to leave a gap which the fire could not leap. A chain of men passing buckets from the conduit would soon quench a blaze. A baker in Pudding Lane went to bed after damping down his fire. Probably a spark caught in the chimney. In the early hours of Monday, September 2 his staircase was in flames and an hour later the fire had spread to the next house. Nobody thought it was unusual. Samuel

Pepys, roused by a maid, returned to bed. But an east wind took the fire to Thames Street where it spread through the wharves, setting alight tallow, corn, spirits and coal. St. Magnus Church went up in flames.

By this time it was a demon. Nobody could cope with it. The hand squirts used to fight fire were ineffective. Fire hooks were better weapons; they could bring a whole house down if a good grip were gained on the roof. But the Lord Mayor was afraid to order the destruction of good houses belonging to citizens who might be influential. Pepys saw everybody attempting to remove their goods from the line of fire 'but nobody attempting to quench it'.

Pepys was a reporter not a firefighter. He watched the flames for a while and then went to tell the king. Charles II was a decisive character at a time like this. He sent a messenger to the Lord Mayor, telling him to 'spare no houses' but to create a gap before the flames. The Lord Mayor had already realised this was necessary but by now the fire was out of hand and the volunteers couldn't demolish quickly enough.

The streets were swiftly congested. They were so narrow that fire fighters, idle onlookers and escaping householders swayed together in a terrible mêlée. Many took to the river, and overladen boats piled with furniture, bedding, kitchen utensils and money boxes moved dangerously across the reddened water. The king and his brother, the Duke of York, came downriver from Whitehall to see what could be done.

Nothing could be done. Pepys got away in a borrowed cart and his nightshirt at four in the morning By now the crowds pressed away from the river as the waterfront was a barricade of flames and the small City gates were crowded.

Londoners had always resented royal interference but Charles II overruled their prejudice. When the fire continued on Monday he sent his brother and the Privy

Two illustrations from a plague poster. Scenes such as these were very real for Londoners in 1665. Corpses were buried at night, unceremoniously. The drivers of plague carts used masks soaked in vinegar to ward off the germs as they worked.

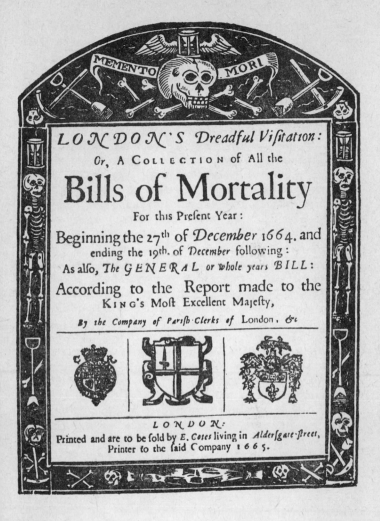

LONDON'S *Dreadful Visitation:*

Or, A COLLECTION of All the

Bills of Mortality

For this Present Year :

Beginning the 27th of *December* 1664. and
ending the 19th. of *December* following :

As also, *The* G E N E R A L *or whole years* B I L L :

According to the Report made to the
KING's Most Excellent Majesty,

By the Company of Parish-Clerks of London , &c

LONDON:
Printed and are to be sold by E. *Cotes* living in *Aldersgate-street*,
Printer to the said Company 1 6 6 5.

*The title page to an official record of deaths during 1665. Defoe
used such contemporary references when he wrote his* Journal of the
Plague Year (1721)—*one of the first reportage pieces in Britain.*

53

Council into the City. Each member of the Council took charge of a section of the burning area, aided by three magistrates, thirty soldiers, the parish constables and a hundred citizens. Militia were sent in from the Home Counties with instruments for demolition and food for the homeless.

But by that evening the Royal Exchange had gone, and the whole of Upper and Lower Thames Streets was burnt out. On the following day St. Paul's, the Guildhall and Christchurch, Newgate, were destroyed; and the fire was spreading across the low slum area which is now Ludgate Circus and New Bridge Street.

Charles took control himself and helped with the fire-fighting. His example rallied the Londoners who tried even more vigorously to fight the flames. He also had no political axe to grind and gave orders for a large gap to be made by blowing up whole streets.

When the fire began to peter out, the thieving had become uncontrollable. There were also rumours of a Catholic plot—the usual bugbear of Stuart London—and of a foreign invasion.

Three fifths of the city had been destroyed when the wind dropped late on Tuesday night. It was the magnificent three fifths—not the new poor areas or fashionable Covent Garden but the whole centre of the City. On the hills above London the inhabitants of the smouldering city lay on the ground surrounded by their possessions and saw a flattened, charred remnant of their homes.

The loss is computed at 3½ million pounds; 13,200 houses, 87 churches, 44 halls of the City companies and the landmarks of the Royal Exchange and St. Paul's were all burnt.

The king was still acting swiftly in the emergency. He supplied tents, presumably from the army, and permission was given to build temporary structures. He commanded all towns to receive the homeless and to allow them to follow their trades. The provincial towns were already being taxed for the relief of Londoners who had suffered in the plague. Charles II was popular in London but not in the provinces. The general fears of political unrest were silenced at once. He rode to Moorfields, where the homeless were camped and quenched the rumours of invasion and plot, assuring the crowd that he would personally care for them.

Slowly Londoners filtered home, setting up sheds on the sites of their houses. Rents became monstrously high in those parts of London that had survived. The City authorities met to reorganise the markets and the business exchange. Labourers were put to work on shift systems so that rubble was being continually cleared; a way was cut through to London Bridge. The Stuarts had always wanted to improve the London buildings. Londoners had at last realised that their home was outmoded, unhealthy and downright dangerous. At last they could rebuild.

By September 10 the first plan to rebuild London was handed to the king. It was closely followed by three others. The first came from Dr Christopher Wren, a professor of astronomy and an eminent scientist. The others were the work of John Evelyn, Captain Valentine Knight and Robert Hooke. Wren's ideas on architecture came from books. His advantage was a scientific outlook. He was already employed as a deputy surveyor under Sir John Denham and six months before the fire the king had asked him to consider the restoration of St. Paul's.

All the plans had good points; they all had geometrical precision. They were not used. Wren's plan, which seems the best, would have entailed a complete redistribution of land. After the fire a survey attempted to register boundaries of properties. Citizens were already grubbing in the ashes to find the foundations of their lost houses. The fire had ruined some of them—speculative landlords in particular—and they wanted to rebuild as quickly as possible. They were not allowed to. Rebuilding was not

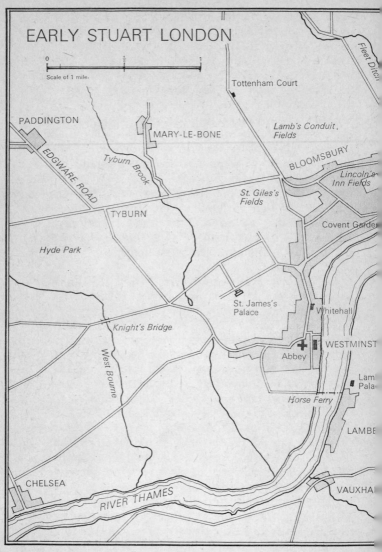

EARLY STUART LONDON

Scale of 1 mile.

Fleet Ditch

Tottenham Court

PADDINGTON

EDGWARE ROAD

Tyburn Brook

MARY-LE-BONE

Lamb's Conduit, Fields

BLOOMSBURY

Lincoln's Inn Fields

St. Giles's Fields

TYBURN

Covent Garden

Hyde Park

St. James's Palace

Whitehall

Knight's Bridge

WESTMINSTER

Abbey

West Bourne

Lambeth Palace

Horse Ferry

LAMBETH

CHELSEA

RIVER THAMES

VAUXHALL

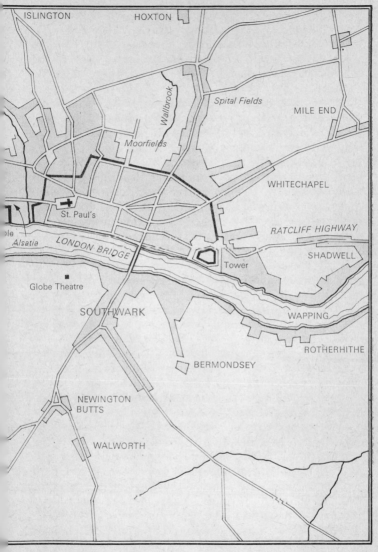

ISLINGTON HOXTON

Wallbrook

Spital Fields

MILE END

Moorfields

WHITECHAPEL

St. Paul's

RATCLIFF HIGHWAY

ole

Alsatia LONDON BRIDGE

SHADWELL

Tower

Globe Theatre

WAPPING

SOUTHWARK

ROTHERHITHE

BERMONDSEY

NEWINGTON
BUTTS

WALWORTH

permitted, although a little restoration to damaged houses was allowable. Fortunately for the authorities it was a bitter winter and no building could be done. The cold weather was little comfort to the homeless living in ramshackle sheds or paying exorbitant rents in untouched suburbs.

Three days after it had been proposed, Wren's plan was rejected probably on the advice of the City authorities. It was too utopian. The king's proclamation of September 10 commanded that houses could only be built of brick and stone in the future. A broad quay was to be built along the Thames between Puddle Dock and Billingsgate. The smoky trades should also be isolated together. Surveyors were appointed, three by the king and three by the City, and drew up the building regulations. In February the building laws were published. They laid down regulations on the height of storeys, the type of elevation, the relationship of floors and street level and the materials of the new houses. To this was added a stipulation that key streets should be 60 feet wide with decreasing breadths according to importance. Alleys were to measure 16 feet across. If houses were not rebuilt within three years the land reverted to the crown.

There were financial problems. Many private citizens appealed for building aid to the king, who had no money himself. A coal tax was levied, which gave some aid and the city found reserves for immediate relief.

New manufacturing grew out of the fire. Brickfields expanded in St. Giles and Moorfields. Workmen flocked into the town to labour at the rebuilding. The six commissioners worked at the new London day and night. Gradually a new city appeared, with wide paved streets, well-proportioned, flat-faced houses and access to main roads from the town. The spires and towers of Wren's churches spiked the skyline round St. Paul's. Wren would be superintending that project for another 36 years.

The Fleet and Alsatia

When the fire so nonchalantly leaped Fleet Ditch and started up towards Fetter Lane, it demolished an area of terrible slums. The Fleet River had flowed into the Thames from Holborn Bridge, which was well up the Farringdon Road. New Bridge Street had been the course of this river, which had become an open sewer. By 1666 the ditch had silted up at Ludgate Circus and on the squelchy boggy area between there and Holborn Viaduct, the very poor had set up ramshackle sheds for dwellings. The state of the Fleet Ditch was an open sore. Since it was just outside Ludgate the City felt little responsibility. The Westminster authorities were not anxious to claim it. Its nearest neighbours were in slum areas, where its condition was hardly noticed.

Apart from the rejected grand design, Wren had two other plans for that part of London. The first, to erect a grand Thames Quay along the burnt-out docks from Blackfriars to Billingsgate, came to nothing. His second scheme was carried out. The river was unsilted and became a waterway. On either side were broad pavements

59

where wagons and coaches could park.

But already this plan was almost outdated. The river was already giving way to the road and the opening up of the Fleet River made very little difference to London traffic. Instead the Fleet became a dumping ground for refuse and its condition deteriorated even more. In 1733 it was filled in again and the main course became an underground sewer.

On the east of Farringdon Street is a Congregational Memorial Hall of 1874. This building is partly on the land once carrying the Fleet Prison, which was demolished in 1846. The Fleet was used for debtors and also for religious intransigents. William Penn was imprisoned here. It was a prison hated less for its austerity than for its sickness rate, which isn't surprising as it overshadowed the Fleet River. Behind it, on the site of the Old Bailey, was another of London's gaols, Newgate Prison.

One of the most interesting, and certainly one of the most frightening, areas of Stuart London lay between Fleet Street and the river. It had once been the monastery of White Friars, and at the dissolution of the monasteries it should have become a useful extension to the city, supplying more room for shops and many factories. However, the criminals moved into Whitefriars. It was an area bounded by Fleet Street to the north, the Fleet to the west, Waterlane (which is now Whitefriars Street) to the east and the Thames on the south. The monastery became a ruin and squatters moved into the area. By 1580 the inhabitants had claimed that they were exempt from the law, as the area was religious ground. They set up a small city within a city, a warren of thieves' kitchens, brothels and fences' shops. In 1608 James I acknowledged and extended their exemption from the law. He may have felt it was a joke against the City authorities, or he may not have realised the possible consequences of his action. The king not only confirmed the inhabitants' right of possession, he granted taxes, franchise and privileges to this secret and self-governing community, heirs to the original Templars and Hospitallers. In 1668 the City challenged these rights but they had no chance of exerting their authority in the Whitefriars area.

Alsatia, as the Whitefriars region was called, became the criminal centre of London; but it also appealed to writers, painters and adventurers who liked to feel they lived in a romantic neighbourhood beyond the jurisdiction of the City.

The Jacobeans made various references to Alsatia. Shadwell even wrote a play called *The Squire of Alsatia,* which describes the inhabitants in the early years of the 17th century.

In the time of James I there was a vendetta in Alsatia. It was the centre for fencing masters, who probably acted as professional bullies when they were not fencing. One of them, Turner, taught a courtier, Lord Sanguire, one of James I's favourites from Scotland. In the foils Sanguire pressed Turner hard to prove himself better than an expert and lost an eye. At the time Sanguire did nothing, but some years later he was asked by the king of France how he had lost his eye and, on being told, Henry IV said, 'Doth the man live?' This seemingly innocent question turned Sanguire into a paranoiac. He considered the matter for some time and then returned to England and hired mercenaries, Gray and Cartier, to kill Turner. They waited several more years and then assassinated Turner in Alsatia. The whole period of considered retribution was about five years.

Gray refused to commit the murder at the last minute and so another assassin enters the story—Irweng. The two murderers called on Turner who was sitting 'in a house in the Fleet which Turner used to frequent'. Turner, drinking with friends, asked them to join him but Cartier and Irweng shot him in the chest, 'so that Turner, having said these words, "Lord have mercy upon me! I

The Squire of Alsatia, the hero of Shadwell's play of the same name, which was as representative of the area as La Bohème *was of Parisian Bohemia. But this resort of criminals could hardly be romanticised in an age when it was a corrupt, red-light district.*

am killed" immediately fell down'. Cartier ran towards Fleet Street and Irweng to the river but Irweng ran into a 'court where they sold wood, which was no thoroughfare' and was seized. Cartier escaped to Scotland. James I issued an order for the arrest of Sanguire and his employees. Cartier and Irweng were hanged in Fleet Street, opposite the great gate of Whitefriars (which is now Bouverie Street). Sanguire was hanged too, but in Palace Yard, Westminster, as befitted a nobleman.

The Inner and Middle Temples (called collectively the Temple) are between Whitefriars and Essex Street. The gateway to the Temple is on the south side of Fleet Street, and was built in 1684 by Roger North. Middle Temple Lane leads from this gateway to the Embankment. Middle Temple and Inner Temple are two of the four Inns of Court. The others are Gray's Inn and Lincoln's Inn. Here law students keep terms, and by dining in hall for a certain number of days in a term they qualify to be called to the bar. Each of the four inns is self-governing.

Middle Temple Hall was opened in 1576. In the Stuart period it acquired a portrait of Charles I. Doors were put in the oak screen in 1671. *Twelfth Night* was performed here for the first time on February 2, 1602.

Both Royalists and Parliamentarians belonged to Middle Temple, and among the most outstanding were Clarendon, the remarkable Royalist historian who was to become Charles II's Chancellor; Pym, the great member of Parliament, who struck the first gesture of insurrection against Charles I; John Evelyn, the dilettante diarist and architect; and William Congreve, the Restoration playwright.

Inner Temple also had famous members in the 17th century, among them John Hampden, Judge Jeffries, and William Wycherley. The atmosphere of the Temple at the time must have encouraged politicians and playwrights. Surviving from the Stuart period are numbers

63

4–6 King's Bench Walk.

The reredos in Temple Church was designed by Christopher Wren and at the west end is a panel of glass through which can be seen the grave of John Selden, the 17th-century antiquary who died in 1654. He had lived in Alsatia.

A 'Templar' was a very real character to the Stuart writers, summoning up a complete picture in the way the words 'spiv' or 'beatnik' or 'hippy' might for us. Essentially he was a young man, interested in literature. After the Restoration, coffee houses were to become popular in Fleet Street, catering for the Templars, who loved to talk above all else. They wrote and criticised and founded a tradition for witty conversation and self-confidence which was to form a background for the wits and writers of the following century.

The first English tragedy *Gorbeduc* had been written in the Temple and a literary coterie maintained this tradition. Between the Temple gate and Temple Bar was The Devil's Tavern, where Ben Jonson held a court of hopeful young writers. In 1687 Messrs. Childs bought it, and it became the premises of the first English bank.

Inner Temple Lane joins Fleet Street opposite the entrance to Chancery Lane. Above the gate is a building of 1610 or 1611, faithfully restored. This has a room called Prince Henry's Room; it is on the first floor and has a 17th-century plaster ceiling and carved oak panelling. Henry was the elder son of James I and was doted on by Londoners. His father seems to have been in awe of him. Henry was intelligent, handsome and athletic, and his younger brother could hardly hope to follow him with any success. When he died from a chill caught while playing tennis, he was deeply mourned. He was seventeen, but politics started early in those days. This room is said to have been his council chamber for administering the Duchy of Cornwall. There was a famous tavern, farther west, The Cock, which was a centre for Jacobean

64

Three famous Stuart Londoners

Above left: *Sir Christopher Wren*
Above: *Inigo Jones*
Left: *Samuel Pepys*

Right: *The effigy of John Donne, a relic of old St. Paul's, now in Wren's cathedral*

Previous page: *The statue of Charles I, cast by Le Sueur in 1633 placed at Charing Cross after the Restoration*

Above: *A representation by Hollar (1649) of the wife of a city dignitar*
Right: *The Banqueting Hall, Whitehall, designed by Inigo Jones. T*
painted ceiling is by Peter Paul Rubens.

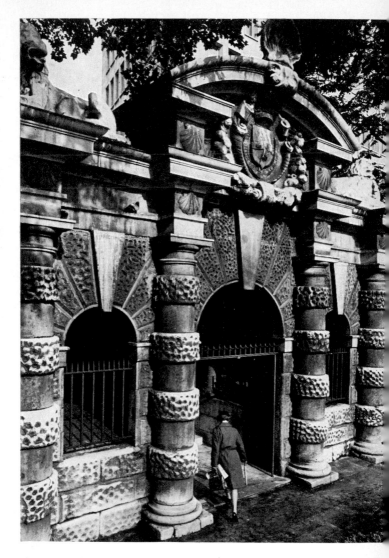

Above: *York Stairs, a watergate (c. 1626) on the Embankment based*
designs by Inigo Jones. It is all that remains of the magnificent town hot
of the 1st Duke of Buckingham.

Right: *The Monument, 202 feet high, which can be climbed by an inter*
staircase.

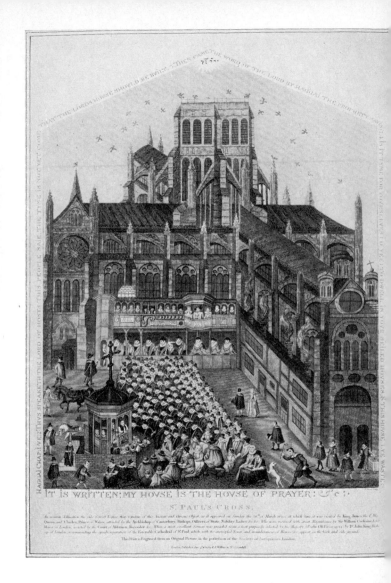

The Bishop of London preaching at St. Paul's Cross before James I, queen, the Prince of Wales and a distinguished congregation.

artists and playwrights. The present pub of that name in Fleet Street is on the same site, but was rebuilt in the late Victorian style. Opposite the entrances to the Temple is St. Dunstan-in-the-West, one of the few churches not destroyed by the Great Fire, though it was rebuilt in 1829. The clock was made in 1671. In the 17th century this area of Fleet Street would have been even more of a bottleneck than it is now, because Temple Bar was another gateway between the City and Westminster.

On the north side of Fleet Street are warrens of courts and alleys, surviving in outline from the 17th century, although most of them have been rebuilt within the last hundred years. In Crane Court, between Chancery Lane and Fetter Lane, the Royal Society held its meetings and kept their museum and library. On the south side of Fleet Street, near Ludgate Circus, is St. Bride's; it was rebuilt by Wren after the Great Fire. In it is a memorial to the Pilgrim Fathers; one of them, Governor Winslow, was a Fleet Street apprentice. Samuel Pepys was born on the south side in Salisbury Court in 1633 and he was christened in nearby St. Bride's. The White Swan now stands on the site of Pepys's house.

Chancery Lane

Isaac Walton, one of the most lovable men of the 17th century, had a home in Chancery Lane in the second house on the left as you travel north. He had a linen draper's shop, although he must have spent most of his time fishing, and writing about fishing. A hosier, John Mason, had half the shop. Soon after 1624 Walton moved two houses up the road, and crossed to the west side, where he opened a milliner's, or sempster's. Strangely, another writer, Abraham Cowley, was born on the west side of Chancery Lane, in the corner house. Cowley was a charming, gentle man, a poet and prose writer of the Interregnum and Restoration. Strafford, the king's adviser who was beheaded in 1639, was also born in Chancery

Lane. The wall of Lincoln's Inn runs along here and Ben Jonson is said to have worked on the original wall as a bricklayer, wielding volumes of Virgil and Horace between handling the trowel.

Fetter Lane is the other street running north and south between Holborn and Fleet Street. It was once the centre for hatmaking but Dryden lived there too. In Charles II's reign the famous Puritan Praise-God Barebones was brought to trial and stated that he had a house in Fetter Lane for which he paid £40 a year.

Holborn can be reached through Shoe Lane, Fetter Lane or Chancery Lane. Its name is a derivation of 'Hole Bourne', marking the site of the Fleet River, which ran through a bourne or hollow. Holborn's most noticeable building is Staple Inn, opposite the entrance to Gray's Inn Road, built in 1586. In the 17th century it was one of the Inns of Chancery, a minor Inn of Court which students would attend before going to one of the four major inns. The building was renovated in the 18th century and badly damaged by a flying bomb. It was restored in 1954.

Silver griffins mark the entrance to the City of London near the junction of Holborn and Gray's Inn Road. On the north of High Holborn is the entrance to Gray's Inn. From 1576 until 1626, Francis Bacon lived in this pleasant, secluded inn. *The Comedy of Errors* was performed in Gray's Inn late in 1594, which is an interesting subject for supposition for those who believe Bacon was Shakespeare. The square of Gray's Inn still has some 17th-century houses, which were damaged during the war. In the gardens are catalpa trees, which are supposed to have been planted by Bacon with cuttings brought from America by Raleigh.

Holborn was a fashionable shopping area in Stuart times, with a great quantity of foreign goods. The 'ton' who lived in Covent Garden or the Strand would visit Holborn to buy gloves, lace, perfumes and leatherwork.

A mountebank or quack doctor of the 17th century. These vagrants,
often with criminal reputations, lived in Alsatia, behind Fleet Street.

It had an air of Bond Street about it which was accentuated by the work of Barbon.

Barbon was probably the first large-scale speculative builder in London. We know that speculative landlords had existed before the Great Fire because of the outcry when their investments went up in flames; but Barbon built his own investments. Nicholas Barbon was not a genteel Frenchman. He was probably the son of Praise-God Barebones, one of the most fanatical members of the Parliamentary party which had sent Charles I to his execution.

However, his son did very well after the Restoration. It had helped that he changed his name, and also that he studied medicine in Holland during the Interregnum. He was an astute businessman. In *London Growing* the author, Michael Harrison, is more unkind: 'He was a rogue and a smarmy rogue; and few who trusted him were not swindled.'

Unlike the later Russells, Barbon had no land to develop but he divided and subdivided what land he could acquire into pint-sized building plots. He then employed workmen to build houses for others or speculative houses for himself on the plots. He developed the best facet of English architecture because he believed in mass production and utilising land—the result was the terrace.

In spite of an outcry from the Benchers of Gray's Inn, Barbon houses sprouted in Holborn, Bedford Row and Red Lion Square. It was the first housing estate and it caused a public clamour. There is a theory that Barbon had to create squares because the Benchers would not allow streets and that the open space was an emergency measure rather than a piece of architectural planning.

The inmates of Gray's Inn invoked Wren and legal aid but Barbon built on. He was always swallowing another parcel of land before it could be reclaimed for a green space or as a king's gift. Barbon's coup was the Harpar Estate, which he bought from Bedford corporation, and he left his indelible stamp on the whole area of Red Lion Square, Theobald's Road, Southampton Row, Great Ormond Street and Gray's Inn Road. Obviously most of Barbon's houses have disappeared or acquired new façades, but the street layout is the one he designed in the 1680s. Barbon marched west. There is one of his houses in St. James's Square, concealed behind a façade of 1725. He went into St. Giles and built over the area to Oxford Street. He replaced some of the City houses which had been destroyed in the fire. His youth in Holland must have influenced his style of red brick with stone facing—grave and reverend houses, which his contemporaries abhorred.

The land round the Inns of Court had been eyed by would-be speculators throughout the century. The Benchers had forestalled building by arranging pleasure gardens through which fashionable Londoners would walk on Sundays. Pepys used his leisure to watch the ladies in Gray's Inn, but later in the century these Inns of Court promenaders became less innocent and a respectable lady wouldn't walk there unless accompanied by her husband.

Lincoln's Inn Fields

Westwards from Chancery Lane, between Holborn and Aldwych, is Lincoln's Inn. This was also a development of the 17th century.

William Newton was a speculator like Barbon, but he operated thirty years earlier. When he began his schemes there was an area of pasture land between Lincoln's Inn and Drury Lane. It was called Fickett's Fields and it had originally been an archery ground. Covent Garden, to the west of this land, had a few houses built by the Earl of Bedford. Beyond Covent Garden was farmland as far as St. Giles, the village which was connected to London by Holborn, and from which ran Tyburn Way (now Oxford Street).

Into this pastoral setting dropped Newton with plans for new houses. Charles I had appealed in vain for brick or stone houses. All his commands and requests had been ignored by Londoners. Newton had no opposition from the king's Commissioners of Building, not only because he would build fireproof houses, but because he would employ the royal architect, Inigo Jones.

In the late 1630s the Palladian style, as translated by Jones, was thought to be the most elegant and magnificent architecture of the age. 'Italianate' houses were being built in the country by nobles; Newton planned a further translation, to reduce the houses in size and set them up in London.

There was universal applause. The king, Charles I, Inigo Jones and the king's connoisseur friend, Lord Arundel, all acclaimed the italianisation of London. Fickett's Fields became a ribbon development known as Lincoln's Inn Fields. Between 1637 and 1643 houses rose in bright red brick, absolutely identical and geometrical, with pilasters in the Corinthian manner. When the Civil War drove the king and his friends from London there was a sharp check to Italianate styles. Advanced architectural ideas were considered decadent and Royalist. And William Newton was dead. His schemes half finished, he had died in 1642.

But when Charles I had granted Newton the right to build 32 houses in Lincoln's Inn Fields he had agreed with the lawyers of Lincoln's Inn that a square should remain leaving an open space for recreation. The Benchers of Lincoln's Inn were as opposed to new building as those of Gray's Inn. They stopped any more building by petitioning Cromwell in 1656, but in 1657 it was obvious that the square could not remain in the half-built state in which it had been left by Newton's death and three characters, Sir William Cowper, James Cowper and Robert Henley, took leases to finish the building.

Numbers 59–60 Lincoln's Inn Fields are a relic of the

work of Newton and Inigo Jones. They were built about 1640 for the Earl of Lindsey. Inigo Jones is supposed to have given the ground of the square the exact dimensions of the base of a pyramid. This seems a remarkable achievement for that period, and a very dubious one.

Lincoln's Inn

In the south-east corner of Lincoln's Inn Fields is an archway which leads into Lincoln's Inn, one of the four Inns of Court. Most of the buildings you pass are 19th-century, but in the south of Lincoln's Inn is New Square, a 17th-century court to the east of which are the Old Buildings; these were here in Tudor and Stuart times. From the Old Buildings you can pass through another opening into a secluded court. On the west side of this Old Square, there is the Old Hall. The Great Hall at Lincoln's Inn was a centre for entertainment and play-acting like the halls of other inns in the 17th century. This building originally dated from 1491 but the south end was added in 1624. The screen is supposedly by Inigo Jones. This ubiquitous architect rebuilt the chapel of Lincoln's Inn, which is on the north end of Old Square. It was built in 1623 and almost inevitably restored by Wren in 1685. The first sermon was preached by John Donne, who laid the foundation stone of the 1623 building. The glass is 17th-century. John Thurloe is buried in the chapel crypt. He was the morose secretary of state to Cromwell who is also supposed to have studied law at Lincoln's Inn for two years. There was a legend that Cromwell was a debauched student, circulated by stories among Lincoln's Inn students. Another student of the period was the famous lawyer, Sir Matthew Hale, who, while he was at Lincoln's Inn, became converted to sobriety. His revelation came when he went on a drinking bout with some other law students one of whom 'went on with his excess, till he fell down in a fit seemingly dead, and with some difficulty recovered'. Like a character in a Victorian novel, Hale responded by praying for help and turning to a serious, unintoxicated way of life.

From this courtyard can be seen the other side of the wall bordering Chancery Lane, which may, or may not, have been built by Ben Jonson. Aubrey, the gossiping 17th-century biographer, says: 'A knight or bencher, walking through and hearing him [Jonson] repeat some Greek names out of Homer, discussing with him, and finding him to have a wit extraordinary, gave him some exhibition to maintain him at Trinity College in Cambridge.' Fuller, in his *Worthies of England*, adds that Jonson had already been at St. John's in Cambridge before he came to work on the wall but that he was obliged to turn to bricklaying through family poverty. Jonson's stepfather was a bricklayer so it seems quite likely that an unemployed student would turn to this work.

There was another Inn of Chancery between Lincoln's Inn Fields and the Aldwych. This was Clement's Inn, which had belonged to the Clare family, from whom it passed to the Inner Temple. It had a well which was celebrated as a meeting place for 'the youth of the city', which suggests it was a haunt for courting couples.

Aldwych was a fashionable area for would-be courtiers, who perched at the end of the Strand like so many birds waiting to fly into Whitehall if affairs looked favourable for them. The various streets leading off it— Arundel, Norfolk, Surrey and Howard—occupy a site once covered by the town house of the Arundel family. It was a wide, low house and in the time of James I it was let to a succession of ambassadors. In the reign of Charles I, Thomas Howard, Earl of Arundel, lived in it, and kept part of his collection of classical statues there. Arundel was a great collector in friendly rivalry with the king, to whom he acted as an artistic adviser. It was he who collaborated with Charles I and Inigo Jones in the scheme to build Lincoln's Inn Fields.

After the Great Fire, Arundel House was a temporary meeting place for the Royal Society, which had given up its usual offices at Gresham College to the Lord Mayor and his council when the Guildhall was burnt down. When they left, old Arundel House came down, and it was replaced by the new streets. These were favourite lodging places for Restoration actresses, pleasantly situated between the river and Drury Lane.

In the south-west corner of Norfolk Street lived William Penn. This eminent Quaker may here have astonished his father in the famous scene in which he appeared before the old admiral in the austere Quaker dress and said 'Friend Penn, how dost thou do?'. Penn's advocacy of the Quaker cause created consternation at court where he refused to take his hat off to Charles II.

Somerset House

Somerset House is on the site of one of the royal palaces, which traditionally belonged to the Stuart queens. When Anne of Denmark, the wife of James I, moved in, she began a tradition of masques and entertainments. She and her court ladies were said to continually appear 'like so many sea nymphs or nereids...to the ravishment of beholders'.

It was in Somerset House that the first squabble took place between Charles I and his wife Henrietta Maria. Later, their marriage appeared idyllic, and it was so as long as the king allowed his self-willed little wife to have her own way. Her demands created so much tension that she is often blamed for the Civil War itself and for the Royalist defeat in that war. Although both events arose out of economic and social pressures rather than any personality, Henrietta Maria did antagonise many of her husband's friends; and she demanded autocratic measures which Charles, who was a reasonable, if weak,

73

man, would never have carried out on his own. Later critics said Charles was infatuated with his wife. In fact he was dominated by her, but when she first arrived in London he did make some effort to control his domestic situation. The queen had arrived with a large French household, which seemed inclined to live very happily in Somerset House. There were repeated grievances, from citizens who were abused and whose bills were not paid, and from English courtiers who were insulted by the French. Finally, Charles went down to Somerset House and calling the French household together, told them to return to France. This caused an uproar. An hour after the meeting, one of the court, Lord Conway, told the French that baggage wagons and horses would be ready for their removal on the following morning. The French procrastinated by saying they had debts in London and couldn't leave.

Charles's patience snapped; he sent a heated letter to his favourite courtier, the Duke of Buckingham: 'I have received your letter by Dic Graeme. This is my answer: I command you to send all the French away tomorrow out of the towne, if you can by fair means ... otherways force them away, driving them away lyke so manie wilde beastes.'

This ensured that there should be no delay. Debts of nearly £50,000 were paid by the king, and one of the most persistent ladies, Madame St. George, was given jewellery worth several thousand pounds to urge her to go.

But the French continued to camp in Somerset House. Many of them had bribed for their positions in the entourage of the young queen, and her mother, Marie de Medicis, was reputed to have accepted the equivalent of life annuities from French courtiers who felt that life in the English court would be worth the investment in the income they might receive. Old Somerset House was in a state of siege, with baggage wagons in the courtyard. Finally, the yeoman of the guard turned them out of the house, and forty coaches set out for Dover, contriving to make the journey last four days and to run up more debts on route.

During this period the front of Somerset House was added by Inigo Jones. Henrietta Maria also had a Catholic chapel built in the Tudor building, and a cloister to house Capuchin monks. This display of Catholic taste so near to the old city caused a certain amount of discontent. Indeed the fight between the Catholic and Protestant court factions had its roots in Henrietta Maria's household, where priests of both denominations once ran a race to the head of the table to say grace. This infuriated Charles I so much that he left the table, taking his wife with him.

After the Restoration, Henrietta Maria made the same journey once more, from exile in France to a court at Somerset House. It must have been a tragic time, for she had loved her husband in spite of their early problems.

When Henrietta Maria returned, the gardens, which lay between the house and the river, were laid out with avenues of trees and a bowling alley. She was not over-happy here; her contemporaries claimed that this was because she hated to see her daughter-in-law, Catherine of Braganza, succeed as queen, especially since Catherine, who had never learned to speak good English, was a retiring woman, made more shy by her husband's sociability and his mistresses.

In time, when she herself was the dowager queen, Catherine also came to live at Somerset House, and left it when William and Mary were on the throne, to return to her native Portugal.

At the end of the garden beside the river was Somerset Stairs, a watergate, also by Inigo Jones, where the poet Edmund Waller lost his dignity. According to Aubrey, Waller was 'made damnable drunke at Somerset House, where, at the water stayres, he fell down, and had a cruel fall.'

In front of Somerset House, on the Aldwych side, was a famous maypole. Before the Civil War, maypoles were common sights, used as meeting places as much as entertainments. This one was pulled down, like many others, by order of Parliament, and although it was replaced, it never had the esteem of the original one. Perhaps the decade without dancing and public entertainment dampened the spirits of Londoners and made them inhibited. The great maypole had been set up by a blacksmith, John Clarges, whose daughter married General Monk, who was to become powerful in the confusion after Cromwell's death and who invited Charles II to return to England. Another pole was set up in 1713 which was very grand, with a gilt weathervane on top, but in 1718 it was finally removed. Times had changed and public amusements were disappearing in a more genteel age. Public executions were popular but public dancing was not.

Places To Visit

Fleet Street and the Inns of Court

How to get there: Go to Ludgate Circus.
By underground: By Circle and District to Blackfriars.
By bus: To Ludgate Circus by 6, 9, 11, 13, 15, 4, 17, 45, 63.
By rail: Blackfriars Station by Circle and District lines or Southern Region.

Walk westwards along Fleet Street from Ludgate Circus. To your left was Alsatia; nothing remains. In the area of Bride Lane was the notorious women's prison, Bridewell. Notice Bouverie Street where Turner's assassins were hanged; St. Bride's, once restored by Wren; Salisbury Court, Pepys's birthplace. Whitefriars Street recalls the monastery. Enter Middle and Inner Temple, called collectively the Temple.

Going north from Fleet Street walk up through Chancery Lane, remembering Walton, Jonson and Cowley, to Holborn, a fashionable 17th-century shopping centre. Either (1) turn right at the top of Chancery Lane and visit Gray's Inn (to the left through Warwick Court or Fulwood Place); note Staple Inn and the top of Fetter Lane. Or (2) turn left in Holborn and cut through a turnstile to Lincoln's Inn Fields and Lincoln's Inn.

Either journey can be made first: or can be made an addition to previous walks by adding Gray's Inn to an exploration of the City, reaching it by way of Holborn Viaduct: or adding the Lincoln's Inn area to a walk through Covent Garden, which was developed at the same time as Lincoln's Inn Fields.

The Strand and Covent Garden

John Clarges was a jolly blacksmith who set up a may-pole and became father-in-law to General Monk, the most powerful man in Britain. He lived in the Savoy where his wife was a washerwoman, some said a barber. The Duchess of Albemarle, as Monk's wife became, was considered very gross and vulgar, but she was a Royalist, and probably prevailed on her husband to invite Charles II to return.

From this description of the Savoy as a home for a blacksmith and his washerwoman wife, you can imagine that it has changed considerably. Where the hotel now stands south of the Strand was an area, called the Savoy, which had been the site of the home of Count Peter of Savoy in the reign of Henry III. This was destroyed during the Peasants' Revolt in 1381 and the area later became part of the Duchy of Lancaster. Henry VII had converted the palace into a hospital for the poor. By the time of Charles II the district of the Savoy was like a small village; the hospital had lost its usefulness. The poor had to apply for admittance to a master whose power had increased so his work was a sinecure.

Charles II turned the building into a hospital for wounded soldiers and sailors. It was also used for religious conferences. We know it had a Gothic gate and a flint wall and because the Strand ran between the Savoy and a great mansion belonging to the Exeters, the road became ridiculously narrow.

Alongside the area once occupied by the Savoy is Savoy Street from which you can reach the Chapel of the Savoy. This is where Samuel Pepys heard Thomas Fuller preach. The historian who wrote *Worthies of England* died from a fever which he supposedly caught in the chapel, in 1661.

In the 17th century the Strand was a road containing the mansions of noblemen and courtiers, whose gardens sloped down to the river. In the reign of Charles I, the country area to the north became a fashionable new quarter, covered by speculative building. Since it was the main road linking the City and the seat of the government, the Strand was always busy. Walking west from the Savoy you will find the Adelphi. Before this area was built by the Adam brothers, it had been a palace of the Bishops of Durham; it then passed to the crown. By Stuart times it was no longer a palace but had become Durham Place, a large mansion with a turreted roof. Raleigh had borrowed it from the crown for a town house. After his death Durham Place must have reverted to the bishops, for the see of Durham finally sold it in 1640 to Lord Pembroke, who rebuilt it during the fever for speculative building which William Newton had aroused by his new estate called Lincoln's Inn Fields. These houses were pulled down for the Adam enterprise in the 18th century.

Beyond the Adelphi is York Buildings where York House once stood. This mansion, which ran between Villiers Street and Buckingham Street, was rebuilt as a splendid town house by the first Duke of Buckingham, Charles I's favourite. The only remnant of its grandeur is the Inigo Jones watergate called 'York Stairs'. There was still a York House after the Restoration, but the second Duke of Buckingham was anxious to profit from his father's possessions and the grounds were turned into the alleys and streets which span the area today between the Strand and the river.

It was at York House, in the second duke's days, that Pepys saw a battle between the households of the Spanish and French Ambassadors. The Spaniards got the better of the French. However, by 1672, the French had taken over York House as their embassy and the Spaniards had gone elsewhere. On April 4 John Evelyn visited the house to look at Catholic wax effigies, which were such a novelty to Londoners that in spite of the anti-Papist climate 'all the city came to see it'.

Beyond the Buckingham lands were those of the Northumberland family, whose house was built on the site of an old hospital, and where Northumberland Avenue now runs. Northumberland House passed for a short period into the hands of the Suffolk family, and so the mansion was known as Suffolk House for a period in the 17th century. Northumberland House was a tremendous building with double ranges of pillars, eight niches in the side and an arched gateway. 'The basement of the whole front contains fourteen niches with ancient weapons crossed within them: and the upper storeys have twenty-four windows, in two ranges, with pierced battlements. Each wing terminates in a cupola, and the angles have rustic quoins.' The building sounds grotesque but the gardens were 'distinguished by simplicity'. There was an avenue of trees to screen the great house from the noisome view and smell of the Thames. Like all the great houses by the Strand, Northumberland House would have its watergate. There was no embankment, and the Thames came up to the lawns of the houses. Some of the gardens were so large one would consider them park land today.

North of the Strand

On the north side of the Strand were more great houses. The Russell family in particular kept great state there and their comings and goings and the minutiae of their household expenses were carefully recorded. They lived in the area now covered by references to their name, which lies between Bedford Street and Bedfordbury in the crosshatching of lanes above the Strand.

On the site of Exeter Street was a mansion belonging to the Bishop of Exeter, and the famous statesman Lord Burleigh had a house in the area. Exeter Street became Exeter Change in the days of William and Mary, a squalid little market of shops and wild-beast shows. It was a speculative venture like the Covent Garden area nearby, and mainly occupied by the shops of milliners and upholsterers.

Between Burleigh Street and Catherine Street was Wimbledon House, a mansion built by Viscount Wimbledon, one of the Cecil family, in the days of Charles I. It was burnt down the day after his house at Wimbledon was blown up. We know this must have happened in the late 1630s, but there's no evidence of whether the viscount was set upon by a group of enemies who ruined his country and his town houses on successive days, or whether it was coincidence.

Leicester Square to Covent Garden

Until the reign of Charles II there were fields in Leicester Square, to which courtiers resorted for duels since they were a pleasant early morning walk from Whitehall. After the Restoration a few houses began to creep into the area and the hunting fields of Soho gradually became a country suburb. There had been a family mansion of the Leicester family in Lincoln's Place, a small lane to the north of Leicester Square, and for a short time the house was owned by Elizabeth of Bohemia.

This remarkable woman was not only the great beauty of her time but had such wit and personality that she attracted followers like a honeypot attracting bees. She was the middle child and only daughter of James I. Shakespeare's *Tempest* was written for her wedding to Frederick, the Elector Palatine in 1616, and she had sailed for Germany as 'Th' Eclipse and glory of her kind', a magnet for the poets and courtiers of the time. Her husband was not to be Elector for long. He was asked to become King of Bohemia and to lead a Protestant insurrection against the powerful Emperor of Austria. Elizabeth and Frederick set up house in Prague but soon after their Protestant army was expelled by the Austrians and the Palatine family became wanderers. Their own electorate disappeared under Austrian rule and they fled to Holland. The English, most particularly the London merchants, adopted Elizabeth's cause as their own, but neither James I nor Charles I was prepared actually to go to war over her. In exile, the Palatines produced thirteen remarkable children. Frederick died young and so Elizabeth brought up her brood on charity supplied by well-wishers. Two of her sons, Rupert and Maurice, came to their uncle's aid during the Civil War, and Rupert became an important figure in Restoration London.

When Charles II returned his beautiful aunt came back to England and, with the aid of her close friend Lord Craven, the house in Leicester Fields was provided for her. She hardly lived there. In February 1661 she died, in the house which ironically overlooked the remains of the Military Yard. This was an academy for riding and fencing, which had been used by her elder brother, James's son Henry, who had died young.

The area between Leicester Square and Covent Garden was sparsely built over. St. Martin's in the Fields had been a small church in Tudor times and it was enlarged in 1607 to make room for larger congregations.

The present church was built in 1721.

The Covent Garden area has to be considered as a whole before you look at individual streets. It has been called 'the first great contribution to English urbanism'. The keynote of the area was provided by the speculative building of the Covent Garden Piazza. This square had the new church by Inigo Jones on one side and on the south, the wall of Bedford House. The Bedfords had begun building in the area before their happy inspiration to improve it aesthetically and economically. Long Acre and Drury Lane were built up with new houses bringing in £500 a year.

The Piazza was built between 1631 and 1635 on the old Covent or Convent Garden, and the Earl of Bedford was granted a royal licence to develop it for £2,000. The Covent Garden which covered the area now containing the market, the theatre and the surrounding streets had become a derelict and uninhabited tract. Inigo Jones designed an elegant cloistered square, one of the most charming architectural ideas ever conceived for London. Eighteen houses were erected; only the relic of one remains, at the corner of Russell Street and Covent Garden. It was leased originally to Sir Edmund Verney, the King's Standard Bearer, who had it on a four year lease for £160 a year.

Inigo Jones also designed houses for Great Queen Street, which was to be called 'the first regular street in London'. The whole motif of these new houses set a classical pattern for London housing terraces with geometrically regular and identical façades. It was similar to that of Newton's development in Lincoln's Inn Fields. In *London Growing* Michael Harrison says: 'It was the disciplinary work of the king and his artistic advisers, imposed upon such men as Newton, which created new standards of taste, and which effectively signed the death warrant of timber framed "cants and jutties" not by showing that brick was more fireproof but

PIAZZA in Coventgarden.

The Piazza of Covent Garden, showing St. Paul's church in the centre, one of the first urban de-
velopments in London and a forerunner of many later schemes. Inigo Jones designed it for the
Earl of Bedford.

by demonstrating that timber-lath-and-plaster was old-fashioned.'

The elegant Italianate styles imposed by Charles I through the work of Inigo Jones were to become anathema during the time of Cromwell when new-fangled building was abolished. When Charles II returned he brought a Dutch influence with him. But Covent Garden was built as an elegant centre and it was successful. For the next hundred years Covert Garden was to be in the fashion and, even when the aristocracy moved west, writers and actors continued to live in the area we connect with fruit and flowers.

Long Acre was one of the streets grievously affected by the plague, which began in this area. At the end of the century 'Ring-Houses' sprang up here, where Whigs and Tories were to argue out their politics in beer-drinking clubs. John Taylor, the Water Poet, kept a pub in Phoenix Alley off Long Acre. Taylor himself reappears on the river, but as a landsman he behaved foolishly. His inn was The Crown, and after the execution of Charles I he changed its name to The Mourning Crown. He was warned that this would be considered insurrection, so he changed the name again to The Poet's Head and hung up his own portrait. Cromwell and Dryden both lived in Long Acre when it was a fashionable new address. In the next century, the streets below Long Acre were to house many great men—Voltaire, Reynolds, Hogarth, Thomas Arne and the fictitious Sir Roger de Coverley.

While the acre was still let as pasturage the church was built for the coming inhabitants on the west side of the market square. St. Paul's, backing onto Covent Garden Market, is a magnificently simple structure. 'The Earl is said to have told Inigo Jones that he wished to have as plain and convenient a structure as possible ... little better than a barn; to which the architect replied he would build a barn, but that it should be the handsomest in England.'

It was built in 1633. In 1798 it was restored after a fire but the east portico is original. The church is filled with the graves of interesting Londoners who lived nearby, among them Samuel Butler, who wrote *Hudibras*, a political novel in verse, and died in 1680; Sir Peter Lely, who died in the same year and who painted, one after the other, the mistresses of Charles II, all looking much the same; William Wycherley, the Restoration dramatist, who died in 1715; and over the west door is a limewood wreath carved by Grinling Gibbons, his own memorial, which was placed there in 1965. He died in 1721.

In the churchyard Robert Car was buried. Car, a favourite of James I, married the divorced young Countess of Essex, who was a beauty but utterly unprincipled. Car and his wife were suspected of poisoning Sir Thomas Overbury, Car's agent. The whole case with its overtones of witchcraft, murder and general immorality was a *cause célèbre* of the Stuart period. Car, who started as a bright-faced page called 'Endymion' by the king, had been projected as a favourite to be a political pawn. The case absolutely discredited him. His daughter married into the Bedford family and so he is buried on their estate in the church his son-in-law commissioned.

From the market, Russell Street runs eastwards to Drury Lane. Here the coffee houses were established before the St. James's area (more usually associated with coffee houses and clubs) was developed. On the corner of Russell Street and Covent Garden was the Hummums. This bath house, which is sometimes called a *bagnio*, was one of the first in Western Europe. It was not only a Turkish bath but also a meeting place and a kind of clinic where 'cupping' or blood-letting was performed on the premises.

On the west side of Bow Street was Will's famous coffee house. This was the salon of the poet John Dryden. Opposite, on the same site as the Hummums, later arose Buttons, which succeeded Will's as the gathering place of poets at the beginning of the 18th century. It was from Will's that Dryden was returning one night when he was set upon in Rose Street by a gang, suspected to have been hired by the Earl of Rochester.

The boy, Alexander Pope, asked to be taken to Will's to see the great Dryden and describes him as 'plump, with a fresh colour'. Later Pope was to declare that he had to avoid Will's and the Russell Street Coffee House as Addison's late hours would do him injury. Will's was nicknamed 'Wits' and political lampoons were created here by courtiers as well as the poets. Licentious Rochester and his equally unstable friend Buckingham were members. One of the taverns in Bow Street, The Cock, was the centre for the most profligate of Charles II's court: 'Sackville, who was then Lord Buckhurst, with Sir Charles Sedley and Sir Thomas Ogle, got drunk at The Cock in Bow Street, Covent Garden, and going on to the balcony, exposed themselves to the company in very indecent postures. At last, as they grew warmer, Sedley stood forth naked, and harangued the populace in such profane language, that the public indignation was awakened; the crowd attempted to force the door, and being repulsed, drove in the performers with stones, and broke the windows of the house. For this misdemeanour they were indicted and Sedley was fined five hundred pounds. . . .'

Where the Covent Garden Opera House stands there were shops in which the elegant beaux of the Restoration bought their clothes, including peruke wigs which could cost £50 or £60 each.

Although the Earl of Bedford gained his licence to hold a vegetable market in 1661 it was hardly used for this purpose until the end of the 18th century. Today the only indication of its previous fashionable eminence is the opera house, St. Paul's Church and a few plain brick houses, relics of the age when a rich nobleman would buy a new town house in Covent Garden.

A coffee house scene. The first coffee houses opened in Fleet Street, and the idea later spread to fashionable Covent Garden.

Places to Visit

The Strand and Covent Garden

How to get there: By underground: To the Temple on
the Circle and District Lines (closed
Sundays); Strand Station on the
Northern Line; Charing Cross on the
Bakerloo, Northern, Circle and District Lines; Aldwych, Piccadilly Line,
rush hours only.

By bus: 6, 9, 11, 13, 15, 60, 77 along
the Strand. To Aldwych by 172, 188,
196, 68, 77, 170 through Kingsway;
from Waterloo Bridge by 4A, 1, 60,
68, 171, 176, 188.

To see both sides of the Strand we charted the walk
from the Aldwych to Charing Cross and back through
Covent Garden.

Notice St. Clement's Dane Church, Arundel, Norfolk
and Surrey Streets going south to the river. On your left
was Butcher's Row, a shameful collection of slum houses.
Somerset House, behind the shops and King's College,
was an earlier building and a royal palace with gardens
to the river. Crossing Lancaster Place enter the Strand.
To the left is Savoy Street, with the Chapel of the Savoy.
From Adam Street to Villiers Street was York House and
beyond it were other mansions and parks. Cross the
Strand, walk back towards the Aldwych. Cut north
through Bedford Street to Rose Street and Long Acre.
Turn right in Long Acre and walk eastwards to Bow
Street. Turn south here to Covent Garden market, the
original Piazza. On the west side of the market is St.
Paul's Church, built by Inigo Jones.

Drury Lane and Lincoln's Inn Fields

The Earl of Bedford had begun his grand design by building a few houses in Drury Lane at the end of the 1620s. By 1670, the lane was one of the centres of fashionable life. The sudden importance of the street emphasises how completely the face of the city was changing, with the old city in disrepute and unfashionable, while new buildings and new town plans were eagerly pursued. The lane was built on land which had belonged to the Drury family. Sir Robert Drury was a patron of John Donne, but at some time in the first decade of the 17th century the Russells of Bedford must have come into the property. While the Drury family still owned the house, John Donne and his wife lived there rent free. Drury was included in the ambassador's retinue to France by wish of James I, and asked Donne to accompany him. Donne was unwilling, since his wife was pregnant and he didn't like to leave her. However, Drury persuaded him and they went to Paris together. While they were there Donne dreamt that he saw his wife at Drury House, passing through the rooms with her hair hanging over her shoulders and a dead child in her arms. The apparition scared Donne so profoundly that Drury sent a servant back to London to find out if Mrs Donne were ill. The servant discovered that she had almost died, and delivered of a dead child at the moment when Donne had his vision. The story was solemnly repeated by Isaac Walton in his *Lives;* extra-sensory perception was an accepted fact among the Jacobeans, to whom it was as familiar as sudden death.

Drury House was bought by William, Lord Craven and later supplanted by a pub called The Queen of Bohemia. This city merchant's son would be considered a millionaire in this century. He spent his father's fortune and his own in maintaining Charles I's unfortunate sister while she was in exile and in bringing up her children.

Craven rebuilt the old Drury House and called it Craven House. He brought his 'Queen of Hearts' here from Holland, and she only moved to her own house in Leicester Fields a few months before she died. Elizabeth left him her personal possessions, including her letters. Craven, who lived to be 89, outlived all the Stuarts he had served, and died in 1697. He had a charming, generous character. After the death of his beloved queen he became an Honorary Colonel of the Coldstream Guards. When there was an uproar over the brothels in Whetstone Park, Craven took charge of the soldiers who quelled the crowd.

Nell Gwynn lived in an apartment in Drury Lane. Pepys records seeing here there: 'May 1st, 1667: To Westminster, in the way meeting many milkmaids with garlands upon their pails, dancing with a fiddler before them; and saw pretty Nelly standing at her lodging's door in Drury Lane in her smock sleeves and bodice, looking upon one. She seemed a mighty pretty creature.'

The theatre had come to Drury Lane before the Restoration. It had been far enough from the City to escape the censure of the authorities, yet close enough to gain an audience. The earliest theatre there was The Phoenix, which had originally been a cockpit. It was a superior small playhouse but it didn't escape the censure of the London Puritans. In 1617 they destroyed it, but it rose from the flames, and performances were to continue there until 1658 when the Puritans closed down all playhouses. It certainly had a great list of 'first nights', for among the productions were Marlowe's *Jew of Malta,* Heyward's *Woman killed with Kindness,* Webster's *The White Devil,* and Massinger's *A New Way to Pay Old Debts.* The company that performed these plays was called the Queen's Servants and had the patronage of James I's wife, Anne of Denmark. This theatre is remembered by Phoenix Alley off Long Acre and Cockpit Alley between Drury Lane and Wild Street.

William D'Avenant boasted that he was Shakespeare's illegitimate son. It is often forgotten that the Stuart public was very much aware of Shakespeare's importance, and D'Avenant's assertion took him a great way at the court of Charles I. He was a playwright himself and he was knighted rather for his organising abilities than for his literary gifts. Before the Restoration, D'Avenant returned to London and attempted a theatrical revival. Since playhouses had been closed by parliamentary action, he attempted to slide past the regulations by producing plays with music, which he presented as musical events rather than plays. In 1656 D'Avenant took over the old Phoenix, renaming it The Cockpit. Various companies exchanged the theatre between them until it was finally taken over by the famous Thomas Killigrew with the King's Company. Killigrew found the old premises too small and inconvenient and pulled down the original theatre, replacing it with a larger one in 1663. It was burnt in 1671 and rebuilt to designs by Wren. Finally it was re-opened in 1674, with a grand production and a prologue by Dryden. This theatre lasted until 1741. This was the original Drury Lane Theatre, and it was called the Theatre Royal since it had belonged to the King's Company of Players under the patronage of Charles II.

It was undoubtedly the most important theatre of the Restoration. It represented the revolution of the theatre, with the emergence of sophisticated social comedies. Vanburgh, Congreve, Wycherley and Farquhar were all writing for Drury Lane, and nineteen of Dryden's plays were produced there. The theatre became a fashionable centre and its new importance accrued from royal patronage. Previous monarchs had the theatre brought to them and performances were made at court or in private houses. But Charles II was the first and perhaps the last approachable king, who would walk about London like an ordinary citizen and who enjoyed the atmosphere of the playhouse.

Throughout Pepys's Diary there are constant reminders of the social consequence of going to the theatre, where he mixed with the mighty, gossiping with the king's mistresses and hearing terrible scandals. He also records the growing importance of actors. Killigrew, the actor manager, was closer to the king than many of his courtiers and interceded for them with Charles. There were two officers turned actors—Hart and Mohun. Hart played dashing parts and caught the attention of the king's favourite, Lady Castlemaine, who plied him with presents. Mohun was a tragedian who suited the heavy parts. Another popular actor was Goodman, who had been sent down from Cambridge and had become a highwayman. Perhaps the most memorable actress was Nell Gwynn who had 'fetched strong waters'—or rather been a barmaid before she became an actress. She was a great comedienne and seems to have been a natural; Dryden summed up her theatrical character in one epilogue, which she sat up to speak as her bearers came to carry her corpse off stage!

'Hold, are you mad, you damn'd confounded dog?
I am to rise, and speak the epilogue.'

Great Queen Street to Lincoln's Inn Fields

You may remember that Great Queen Street was included in Inigo Jones's original plans for the new urban area around Lincoln's Inn Fields. It was built up about 1640 and received its name in honour of Charles I's wife, Queen Henrietta Maria, which underlined its elegance. The north side of Lincoln's Inn Fields was called Holborn Row, and from its west end Great Queen Street ran into Long Acre. South of Lincoln's Inn Fields, the St. Clement's Dane area stretched to the Strand by way of Butcher's Row, a squalid area which no longer exists. This whole district from Covent Garden market to Lincoln's Inn Fields was a conglomeration of new streets in the 17th century. Leigh Hunt says: 'Great Queen Street, in the time of the Stuarts, was one of the grandest and most fashionable parts of town.' Its association with the Lincoln's Inn area is confirmed by Horace Walpole saying that Kneller, the Restoration portrait painter, 'lived at Great Queen Street, Lincoln's Inn Fields'. His neighbour was another famous Restoration character, Doctor Radcliffe. Walpole says: 'Kneller was fond of flowers and had a fine collection. As there was great intimacy between him and the physician, he permitted the latter to have a door into his garden; but Radcliffe's servants gathering and destroying the flowers, Kneller sent him word that he must shut up the door. Radcliffe replied peevishly, "Tell him he may do anything with it but paint it." "And I," answered Sir Godfrey [Kneller], "can take anything from him but physic".'

Kneller had graduated to Great Queen Street. His addresses suggest his rise in eminence: Durham Yard, the Strand, Bow Street and finally the house with a flower garden. He was an immensely vain man whose portraits hardly impress us now, for although his faces are reasonably human he portrayed wooden figures. His circle knew that by flattery they could win paintings. Later, in the time of Queen Anne, Dr Radcliffe was to fall in love, late in life, and his affair caused a season's scandal. His collection founded the Radcliffe Library at Oxford.

Another interesting inhabitant of Great Queen Street was Lord Herbert of Cherbury who was one of James I's courtiers and one of the first men in England to write his autobiography. He was highly intelligent, hot-headed, interested in science and vainglorious.

The meaner side of London was not blotted out by the new elegance, or perhaps the new elegance attracted vice. Whetstone Park, which runs along the top of Lincoln's Inn Fields, was linked up to Great Queen Street before the development of Kingsway. Here the criminals lived who preyed on the Covent Garden inhabitants.

The types of criminals were listed by Malcolm in *Customs and Manners of London from the Roman invasion to the year 1700*, quoted by Leigh Hunt. There were 'Anglers' who poked sticks through windows and picked up valuables on a hook; 'Rufflers' who dressed up as old soldiers to beg, crying: ' 'Tis a sad thing that an old crippled cavalier should be suffered to beg for maintenance while a young cavalier . . . should ride in his coach.' There were 'Wild Rogues' who not only committed burglaries, but also passed through churches and theatres cutting off gold buttons. 'Palliards' were women who employed children to beg with them, covered with artificial sores. 'Fraters' sold forged patents and 'Whip Jacks' bound up their limbs to appear disabled when they begged. The most colourful and terrifying must have been the 'Abram' men who pretended to be mad and who pounced through the streets in fantastic clothes, uttering wild cries, and picking pockets as they went.

Below Lincoln's Inn Fields was another tributary from the Covent Garden area, which is now separated from it. This is Portugal Street, where the other important Restoration theatre stood. This was the Duke's, named after Charles II's brother, the Duke of York, who was to become James II. Although generally called 'the Theatre in Lincoln's Inn Fields', Hunt says that there were in fact two successive theatres. The first was in a tennis court in Clare Market and the actors who took this theatre had been playing at The Red Bull, presumably in the neighbourhood, until the Restoration. This group moved over under Killigrew to form the King's Company at Drury Lane. But the Duke's Company, headed by D'Avenant, moved to Portugal Street in 1662 from Salisbury Court in Fleet Street. This company stayed in Portugal Street until 1671, then moved back to the Fleet Street premises. No Restoration company regarded its premises as permanent, and as the theatre became more important they were continually enlarging the playhouses and moving to new 'digs' while the renovations were made.

The Duke's Theatre in Portugal Street was as popular as the King's in Drury Lane. It had its own scandals and fracas, including one between the Killigrews and Rochester and Buckingham.

One of the best actors of the company was Kynaston, who must have been one of the last men to play a woman's part. He was so handsome that the court ladies competed to have him ride in their coaches. Betterton performed at the Duke's Theatre. He was the Irving of the Restoration stage and was considered the best Hamlet of the period. One of his fellow actors, who played the ghost to Betterton's Hamlet, was so amazed at Betterton's look of horror at seeing the ghost that he was struck dumb himself and unable to go on with the play.

Clare Market, below Portugal Street, was also part of the new development. It had been Clement's Inn Fields, and the Earl of Clare speculatively built on it in 1657.

The walk described at the end of this chapter links with the previous journey along Fleet Street and up into the Inns of Court. In the earlier walk you can see how the old city is left behind and the Newton expansion into Lincoln's Inn Fields gives the first hint of the urban development to come.

By walking in the opposite direction from the Long Acre and Russell Street part of Covent Garden, you can see how the twin cities linked up with the urban development of the Garden. The Piazza of Inigo Jones is the first square in London, and it is a sign of things to come. The top-heavy Elizabethan buildings which can still be seen in Holborn are a memorial to the London before Charles I, but the elegant town houses of Covent Garden were to supersede them entirely.

Places To Visit

Drury Lane and Beyond

How to get there : Drury Lane can be reached by the same routes as the Aldwych plus :
By underground : To Covent Garden, Piccadilly Line (closed on Sundays) or Holborn, Piccadilly and Central lines.
By bus : From Shaftesbury Avenue to the north, 19, 22, 38; or Charing Cross Road in the west, 1, 24, 29.

Drury Lane runs north from the Aldwych to High Holborn. Notice Great Queen Street, Russell Street, Newton Street (named after the builder); the Theatre Royal, a successor to the King's Playhouse, Dryden and Betterton Street are named after local notables.

Cross Kingsway, remembering Covent Garden's link with the other side of this road. Go through any entrance to Lincoln's Inn Fields. Notice where Whetstone Park was to the north and Portugal Street to the south.

Charing Cross, Whitehall and St. James's

The story of Charing Cross is told in an earlier book in this series. It marked the resting place of the body of Edward I's wife, Eleanor. It was also a signpost for Londoners. If St. Paul's was a focal point for the City of London, Charing Cross was a focal point for the newer City of Whitehall and Westminster. In Tudor days Charing Cross was linked with the City by the Strand, a street of great houses. It joined Whitehall, which was like a village street with an odd assortment of houses set here and there in gardens. Haymarket and Spring Gardens were country lanes, and what is now Whitcomb Street was Hedge Lane. It is said that in Elizabeth's reign you could walk from the lane now called Pall Mall to Hampstead without passing a house. This was the pastoral end of London.

St. Martin's in the Fields was a village church. The cross at Charing Cross was destroyed during the Reformation. The statue of Charles I was placed there after the Restoration. It is said to be the most beautiful equestrian statue in London. It was cast in bronze for the king's friend, the Earl of Arundel, who was involved in Newton's schemes and whose house in the Aldwych was so full of treasures. It was made by Hubert Le Sueur in 1633. After the execution of Charles I the statue should have been broken up, but a brazier, John Rivet, took it away and showed the Parliamentary soldiers pieces of bronze purporting to come from the statue. Rivet sold many mementos to Royalist sympathisers, particularly knives and forks, which were bought secretly at a high price by the mourners. But after the Restoration, Rivet suddenly produced the whole statue, which he had hidden.

Before he returned the Le Sueur bronze there were cruel executions on the site of the statue. In the 17th century there was still a taste for terrible vengeance. The last public executions at Charing Cross were of Harrison, Scrope, Jones and Peters who had been in the council that condemned Charles I. They were hanged, drawn and quartered. But the event must have been too much for Charles II, who afterwards had all executions done at Tyburn, well away from Whitehall.

The Admiralty was originally Wallingford House, which belonged to the second Duke of Buckingham, after he had sold York House, his father's mansion in the Strand. He was one of the most dissolute courtiers of the Restoration. Sir Walter Scott says of him: 'The Restoration put into the hands of the most lively, mercurial, ambitious and licentious genius who ever lived the sum of £20,000 a year, to be squandered in every wild scheme which the lust of power, of pleasure, of licence, or of whim, could dictate to an unrestrained imagination.'

Buckingham had talent and wit and had no idea how to use them. He influenced Charles II in politics at the beginning of his reign and soon his meddling caused vicious repercussions. Buckingham ran through his money and his popularity at a tremendous rate.

Locket's ordinary stood at Charing Cross; its site is

unknown. In the 19th century the Northumberland Avenue Coffee House was supposed to mark the place. We don't know if the present Coffee House is on the same site. Locket's was managed by a woman, Mrs Locket, who evidently exchanged banter with her customers, who included Vanburgh and Sir George Etherege. Vanburgh immortalised her coffee house by making it the resort of Lord Foppington in *The Relapse*.

Spring Gardens run between Whitehall and Cockspur Street. This was a secluded residential area, newly developed in the reign of Charles II. His cousin Prince Rupert lived there; he also had a house in the Barbican, part of the city, displaying the changing taste for fashionable areas. After the Restoration the prince, who had been a soldier and a sailor, became a scientist, a founder of the Royal Society and a promoter of the Hudson's Bay Company, which opened up Canada. John Evelyn visited him to discuss scientific projects and had the prince's discovery of mezzotint engraving explained to him.

Scotland Yard

In the 17th century Scotland Yard was a yard, but it was large enough to hold Well's Coffee House. Milton had worked in an office here when he was employed by Cromwell; and Beau Fielding died in a house in this close.

Fielding was a beautiful man, described as a cross between Hercules and Adonis. He went into exile with James II, but not before he had shown his beauty to London by riding about in an open tumbril, cut low at the sides to show off his exquisite figure, attended by two footmen dressed in black and yellow. Steele records that when the boys of Westminster School laughed at him 'Handsome' Fielding called out 'have you never seen a man before?' and when one replied he hadn't seen one like Fielding, the Beau gave him a crown and thanked him. He was a pathetic figure in his old age, when, after returning to England, he annoyed Swift by trying to gain attention among ladies by displaying the wounds in his chest—'but they all fell a-laughing'. He also called for his tea by beating a drum, and summoned his valet to shave him with a trumpet call. There must have been a streak of insanity in beautiful Beau Fielding which went unnoticed in his own time.

Further down Whitehall, on the left-hand side as you walk south, is the Palace of Whitehall. All we have left is the Banqueting Hall, designed for Charles I by his favourite architect, Inigo Jones.

The Palace had been York Place, the seat of the Arch-bishops of York and it was left as a magnificent house by Wolsey. When Henry VIII took possession he expanded the palace to St. James's Park. On the right-hand side, where the Horse Guards stand, was the Tilt Yard and behind it a mass of houses and gardens comprising the palace.

It's customary to think of the court of James I as a centre of buffoonery and pedantry. James had some interesting courtiers. One of them was Sir John Harring-ton, a witty writer who translated Ariosto and invented the water-closet. James loved hunting as well as gaming and in his time the parkland west of the palace was filled with huntsmen and chases. James had notable favourites. He also had buffoons: Sir Edward Souch, who was a master of the indecent story, and his friend Sir John Finet, as well as George Goring, who once arranged a tilting match between two fools riding pick-a-back on footmen's shoulders. James drank 'not ordinary French and Spanish wines, but strong Greek wines', which affected him rapidly, and he was frequently carried off to bed drunk.

James was of medium height and plump; his clothes increased his ungainliness for they were padded and puffed. His eyes were large and rolling and his beard was thin. He had an impediment which made him salivate. Apparently he never washed his hands but wiped them on a damp napkin. His legs were weak, which made him lean on other people. However, James was a real wit if he needed to be, loyal to his friends and with some very genuine learning.

James's wife, Anne of Denmark, was the lady who appeared at Somerset House in a variety of costumes. She loved masques and celebrations and seems strangely isolated from the more morbid aspects of the court. The most imposing child of these two was probably Henry, the Prince of Wales, whose council room has been mentioned in the section on Fleet Street. Henry died young and his brother became Charles I. Elizabeth, their daughter, was the beautiful girl whose marriage produced *The Tempest* and many poverty-stricken, lively children. These children knitted European royalty together in a complicated pattern; Elizabeth's youngest daughter carried the English crown to George I for she was the only eligible Stuart left with children after the death of Queen Anne.

Charles I was a grave young man of natural good taste, who had wanted to enter the Church and who would have been happier if Henry had lived. He enjoyed the company of aesthetes, poets and artists. His political weaknesses are well known.

After the first spurt of fury at the French hangers-on, he not only accepted his French wife, but allowed Henrietta Maria to ride rough-shod over him. She also loved masques, but she seems to have had more natural grace than her mother-in-law, Anne. The masque master who emerged in the court of James I was Ben Jonson, and his partner was the young Inigo Jones, who first appears as a designer of sets and costumes for the masques at Whitehall.

Masques were the foundation of ballet and opera. They were singing entertainments in which courtiers, dressed in extravagant costumes, performed stately dances. Henrietta Maria enraged the London citizens and the Puritans by dancing in them on Sundays. The essence of the masque was its amateur quality. Professionals would compose, design and coach the players, but these had to be courtiers. It was the first signal of equality at court, for Charles treated Inigo Jones, Ben Jonson and the masque players as friends. He was too reserved to be oversociable, but his son Charles II may have absorbed some idea of the value of commoners when he was an infant in charge of his tutor, Dr William Harvey, who discovered the circulation of the blood.

In the decision to make London Italianate and fireproof, Charles I didn't neglect his own house. He commissioned the Banqueting Hall, which was to be the beginning of a new Whitehall Palace, and he brought Peter Paul Rubens from the Low Countries to paint the ceiling for the high cost (in those days) of £3000.

This Banqueting Hall stood on the site of an Elizabethan hall of 1581, in which *Othello* is believed to have been performed for the first time in 1604. In 1605 the building was rebuilt and in 1612 the unfortunate Queen of Bohemia was betrothed to Frederick, Elector Palatine in its main hall.

The Jacobean Banqueting Hall was burnt down in 1619 and Inigo Jones designed the present building for the king. It was finished in 1622 and shows how influential the young Charles already was in architectural matters; it should have formed the hub of a grand design for a palace covering 24 acres and stretching from the river to St. James's Park. This was the first Palladian building in England, for Jones was influenced by the Italian classical architect Andrea Palladio.

The staircase annexe on the left was added in 1798 and the bust of Charles I which is there marks the place where he walked out onto the scaffold in 1649. The quiet execution on January 30 was felt to be the beginning of democracy. The enormous crowd who watched it saw the

The execution of Charles I. On a cold January day the English committed regicide, leading the way for the republics of later generations. This one would last just over a decade.

king step out on to a platform, nervous that he might shiver with cold since he was in his shirtsleeves and that this might be construed as fear. He tried to speak but his words were blown away in the wind. With one blow England hoped to be free. It had in fact changed one totalitarian regime for another. In the 17th century, in a land still emerging from serfdom, it was impossible to have a government of the type we accept today.

After Charles I's execution, Cromwell inherited White-hall Palace. Strangely enough the grand allegorical paint-ings of *The Apotheosis of James I* and *The benefits of his Government* with *The Union of England and Scotland* were allowed to remain. One imagines that Cromwell was impatient of his surroundings and hardly noticed them. He lived here until 1658, during which time John Milton was his secretary; it was here that he refused the crown and here that he died. In 1649 Parliament had decided that Whitehall, with Hyde Park and other royal grounds, should be made into recreation areas for the public, but by 1651 Parliament decided 'that Hyde Park be sold for ready money'. They can't have found a buyer but a lessee, for in 1653 John Evelyn found he had to pay to go through the park. Cromwell often drove out in Hyde Park from Whitehall.

After the Restoration, Whitehall became a centre for court intrigue. The Whitehall of Charles II must have been rather like the court of his cousin at Versailles, full of people waiting to be noticed, longing to speak, anxious for profit. Horace Walpole thought that Louis XIV imitated the court of Charles I in having a new palace designed for him, and in attempting a controlled hierarchy about the court and some regulation in it; Charles II was less formal.

His court was considered dissolute and extravagant by the Puritans, yet many of the excesses of his courtiers seem to have taken place outside Whitehall. He had three confidential gentlemen—Chaffinch, Prodgers and

Bramket, who vetted visitors and probably had their palms greased by them. They were Grooms of the Chamber, not noble but servants.

Charles II was a nervous man, afflicted by both gaiety and tragedy. His exile and his hard times had given him a common touch, which made him popular. In his continual round of pleasures and mistresses, there is a sort of neurosis. He was witty, sociable and luxurious. His apartments at Whitehall were filled with dogs and clocks. His wife, Catherine of Braganza, is popularly supposed to have had a harsh time; yet most European rulers kept mistresses and few could have been as affable as Charles II, for he protected her from teasing and accompanied her on social occasions. Charles II was a restless tenant of Whitehall; he would pass from room to room, gossiping. He walked in Pall Mall or St. James's, and could be freely approached by Londoners there. His mistresses had lodgings in Whitehall, with gardens and balconies; and there the king's bastards were brought up, close to the possessions they could never claim. The Duke of Monmouth was one, who was a gay spark in the palace. The courtiers were lively and not all were the sots Victorian historians liked to portray; there were Dryden, Wren, Clarendon and Edmund Waller, as well as the bucks, Buckingham, Rochester, Etherege and Sedley.

The revelry ended when Charles II died in 1685. James II was a dull man who lived in his mother's shadow. He had hoped to change so much in his brother's lifetime and he had become a threat to Londoners. After the Monmouth rebellion had been put down ferociously and after attempts to introduce Catholicism, James became a cynosure of hatred. In December 1688 he fled silently from Whitehall and his son-in-law William III was invited to become king of England.

St. James's

The park was a game reserve which should have been overlooked by the rebuilt Whitehall Palace. Charles I crossed it on a cold morning on his way to execution, but Charles II made it popular. He walked through it briskly in the mornings, so fast that his courtiers fell behind. It was a swampy area, with a few ponds and trees when he arrived, but he began to improve it. There is a legend that he invited Le Nôtre over from Versailles to advise him on laying it out; but there is another tale that Le Nôtre came and refused to alter its rural simplicity.

Charles had the Mall laid out as an avenue with four lines of trees. Here he would play pall-mall. This was a game in which a ball was struck with a mallet through an iron arch—rather like croquet. The nobility built houses on either side of Pall Mall—an adjacent alleyway for the game. A canal was made by linking the little ponds. It was 100 feet long and 28 feet wide and in it Charles would swim, watched by his subjects.

The area to the north of St. James's Park was marked out for development as the town spread westwards. Now that Whitehall Palace was a real social centre all the purveyors to the court wanted to set up shops in the district, and the hangers-on wanted to live nearby. The nobles found that a walk from the Strand side of the area was less fashionable than a walk from the north-west. The Covent Garden Piazza had set the mode. The Earl of Southampton had begun to build up Bloomsbury. The Earl of St. Albans, Henry Jermyn, began his own development in St. James's. He suggested that a fashionable area would barricade off the 'low' markets and keep the area filled with high-class neighbours. Charles II gave him a lease of the land to 1721. The English aristocracy no longer needed vast mansions and parks in town. They had them in the country and St. Albans reasoned, rightly, that they would be happy with narrow terraces like those round Covent Garden. It was an area of small

107

streets and a main square, originally with an ornamental pool in the middle; from this centre one street connected with Wren's new church in Piccadilly and other streets connected with a shopping centre, St. James's Market. The main square was built in 1684.

Seeing how well Southampton and St. Albans were doing out of their speculations, other gentlemen imitated them. Sir George Downing bought a marshy tract between Whitehall and the river, and with drainage he did very well, for Downing Street was made up of four houses, built on bog, which are still standing.

A Colonel Panton won money at cards and bought land between the Hay Market and Leicester Fields; he built a street there on the shrewd advice of Christopher Wren. Poor Sir Thomas Bond speculated and lost; Bond Street was too far north, 'out in the sticks'. Frith, Clarges and Jones invested in land on which they built Frith Street and Clarges Street. One imagines Jones Street sounded too common.

One of Wren's master-masons, Abraham Storey, invested the money he had made after the Great Fire in a stretch of land called Storey's Gate, which runs between Westminster Abbey and Birdcage Walk.

The whole area was ripped apart. Between 1665 and 1690 it must have been impossible to walk in the Whitehall and St. James's area without tripping over newly laid foundations, being assailed by bricklayers and masons, or coming upon a wealthy landlord considering plans with an architect.

Places To Visit

Charing Cross, Whitehall and St. James's
How to reach it : Travel to Trafalgar Square.
                 By underground : To Trafalgar Square

on the Bakerloo Line; or to Strand, Circle
and District lines; or to Leicester Square,
Northern Line.

By bus: From Whitehall: 3, 11, 12, 24,
29, 39, 88, 53, 59, 77, 127, 134, 159, 163,
168. From the Strand: 6, 9, 11, 13, 15,
60, 77. From St. Martin's in the Fields, 1,
24, 29, 127, 134.

By rail: Charing Cross by Southern
Region.

Start from the statue of Charles I at Charing Cross.
Look down Northumberland Avenue, site of Northumberland House and Locket's Coffee House. In Whitehall, notice Scotland Yard, the Banqueting Hall, on left
going south; on right Spring Gardens, the Tilt Yard, now
Horse Guards, and the Admiralty once Wallingford
House, home of the second Duke of Buckingham. Remember Downing Street was built for speculation on
marshland. Cut through westwards to St. James's Park
walking along by the water where Charles II used to
bathe. Note the Mall. Go up the Duke of York's steps,
turn left to Pall Mall and then second right into St.
James's Square. From here you can explore the London
developed after the Restoration: Charles II Street,
Jermyn Street, St. James's Street, and so on. It's dubious if
any of the early houses remain although they may be
disguised under newer façades. If you have enough
energy, you can strike eastwards again (after looking at
St. James's Church by Wren, in Piccadilly), down Lower
Regent Street, through Panton Street (Colonel Panton's
development on the advice of Wren) and across Whitcomb Street (the original Hedge Lane) into Leicester
Square; this was hardly a square with only one great
house—Leicester House—and a few early town houses
round the square, which had been laid out in 1635 but
not fully developed.

The London James left

The River and the Suburbs

The London James II left had altered radically from that which his grandfather entered eighty-five years before. In one lifetime London had become a capital instead of a village. The old city, gradually emerging from the burnt-out ruins of the fire, must have seemed like another town to the busy chattering court followers of Whitehall. In Elizabeth's day they would have visited it daily to buy clothes, to hear news, or to listen to sermons at St. Paul's Cross. Now they need not; they had their own centres—Covent Garden or the new St. James's.

The greatest change was displayed in the architecture. The tiered wooden or plaster buildings, top-heavy, dark and haphazard rather than designed, had been replaced by brick houses with stone facings. The regulations on building after the fire had been adhered to, although the houses had sprung up in their old plots so that the streets might have the same layout, but they had a very different appearance. They were wider and the houses were regular in design with porticoed doorways and long windows. The private gardens were disappearing under bricks and mortar.

The people had changed. They were sophisticates. London had its political chance; its Puritan conscience had an opportunity under the Interregnum and it hadn't worked out. It was true that the maypoles had gone, but the playhouses were more popular than ever. The court was Frenchified—many of its members had been exiled on the continent and now they looked eastwards for fashions and ideas. The City merchant was a figure of fun to the aristocrat, who had royal concessions to bring in money, and who lived in a new house in the St. James's district.

For now there was a 'mode', a social climate which was very different from that of the Tudor times. The Elizabethan, and even the Jacobean gallant, went his own way. He dressed elegantly and colourfully to please himself; his manners were the same. Stratifications were loose. The great nobles at the court of Elizabeth had gone to the play or to bearbaitings with the common herd. But by the end of the century, pastimes were being stratified along with the people who pursued them. The world of investment—banking, company business and speculation—had brought a moneyed upper middle class to town who lived off capital and followed fashion. The plays of Vanburgh, Wycherley and Congreve portrayed a new society, where clothes and manners were all important.

If times had altered the London character and the wealthy City merchant was outdated, what of the oldest centre of the city?

The Thames had been the main highway of London, a focal point for great nobles and city burghers. Now it suffered a decline.

There were still Frost Fairs. They were to continue until 1814, and as late as 1820 people would walk on ice feet deep in the coldest part of January. This festivity on

The Great Frost Fair of 1683, when the Thames was frozen in places to a depth of 20 feet and shipping became ice-bound.

the water was made possible by old London Bridge, which was pulled down during the late Regency. The groaning old bridge was held up by heavy columns to support the buildings on it and carried a wide road to enable traffic to enter the city. It effectively dammed up the river and the water flowed more slowly above it. When the thick frosts came the sailing ships would be frozen in port and the rest of London would come out on to the ice to celebrate. The most famous frost was that of 1608. Although it is a novel, *Orlando* by Virginia Woolf contains the best description of the Great Frost. (Incidentally, Mrs Woolf must have had her dates mixed. At the time James had already been king for five years.)

'But while the country people suffered the extremity of want, and the trade of the country was at a standstill, London enjoyed a carnival of the utmost brilliancy. The court was at Greenwich and the new king seized the opportunity that his coronation gave him to curry favour with the citizens. He directed that the river, which was frozen to a depth of twenty feet and more for six or seven miles on either side, should be swept, decorated, and given all the semblance of a park or pleasure ground, with arbours, mazes, alleys, drinking booths etc., at his expense . . . Here and there burnt vast bonfires of cedar and oak wood lavishly salted, so that the flames were of green, orange and purple fire. But however fiercely they burnt, the heat was not enough to melt the ice.'

Taverns and ordinaries were set up and did a roaring trade. Barbers erected little tented shops and the boys came to play football. While the Londoners danced, skated, got drunk and bought ribbons from the decorated stalls, and while great braziers were set up on the ice to warm the passing skaters, the people whose livelihood depended on the river suffered a depression. Watermen were laid off work, cargoes could not be unloaded, trading ships could not sail. What was a holiday for most

Londoners was hardship for a minority.

In 1648 John Evelyn described the traders on the ice-bound Thames, where regular shops had been set up as well as a printing press, which issued souvenir slips, headed 'The Thames', with names, addresses and dates, at sixpence each. On January 9, 1649 he walked from Westminster to Lambeth on the ice.

But if the Londoners turned out in a frost it was for the novelty. They still used the river for transport, but less and less. The watermen of the Thames were vigorous, truculent and full of personality; one imagines they developed into 'characters' like modern New York cab drivers. Their 17th-century laureate was John Taylor, the Water Poet. He claimed that there were 40,000 watermen in London. This is an exaggeration, but there were enough to keep the river covered with their craft, from normal row boats to fast skiffs, which specialised in hastily skimming through between the other boats. There were also fishermen engaged on the Thames, and their catch formed a good part of the Billingsgate trade.

The watermen used wherries, which had six or eight oars and a canopy to protect the customer from bad weather. The fares were quite high—6d from the Strand to Westminster, 2s 6d return from the Strand to Chiswick. Many nobles had their own wherries. The watermen would stand by the slips leading to the river and cry 'oars, oars' to passers-by to gain trade. This shocked one French visitor, who thought it was an invitation to a brothel.

Most foreigners loved the novelty of the boats on the Thames. It had its own sights. In 1617 Busino visited *The Golden Hind*, which had been permanently moored on the Thames, but it had been terribly despoiled by sightseers, who had taken so much timber away that it was 'looking like the bleached ribs and bare skull of a dead horse'; within a few years it had disappeared, the prey of trophy hunters.

Taylor, the Water Poet, was of some consequence. He arranged a water pageant in 1613 for the betrothal of the Princess Elizabeth. But he directed most his energy into invectives against road transport, for as the century wore on, boats were used less, except for journeys across the river. As trade diminished, the theatre owners were blamed for re-siting their theatres on the north bank.

In the 17th century the banks of the river were covered by gardens and meadows. Pepys tells of the plight of a friend who tried to cross the river and lost his way in the mist, discovering the shore with 'flags and reeds'. One of the consequences of the pastoral river banks was a danger from sudden flooding in the days before embankments. Wren had realised that some wall was necessary and made provision for it in his design for London. But since the design came to nothing, the embankment wasn't built until 1864.

London Bridge

The bridge had been there, in some form, since 1014, and by the 14th century it was established as a shopping centre, with 138 tenants. The cost of maintaining the bridge was fairly high, since it carried all the traffic from the south. It was supported by piers, which in turn were protected by 'starlings' or wooden platforms to fend off accidents. Shooting the bridge was a feat among watermen, since the rush of water through the piers was made more powerful by the 'starlings', which had to be negotiated in the churning release of water. The bridge could be damaged by ice, or barges ramming into the piers. Sometimes there were fires up above on the bridge. In 1666 a third of the buildings were destroyed by fire spreading from the shore.

The noise and bustle round London Bridge was increased by Peter Morrice's water wheel, which was under one of the arches. The shops on the bridge were considered to have an advantageous position. They attracted travellers from the south—the first London shops they were to see, and they seem to have been tourist shops, for drapers and milliners were there as well as ordinaries and aleshops.

Traitors' heads were exposed on the bridge, which added to its tourist attraction. In the 1750s the shops were to be demolished, the houses removed and alcoves were made along the bridge at intervals. It lost its character but it was much safer.

London Streets

During the 17th century the traffic from the river went into the streets. The streets themselves had been widened after the fire but they were no less congested. In 1623 John Taylor wrote a pamphlet with the bitter title *The World Runs on Wheels,* and so it did. By the end of the century the roads of London were suffering from the volume of traffic. There were deep ruts where coach wheels had run for 75 or 80 years and, like tramlines, they had to be followed or the jolting would throw passengers out of the vehicle. There was a parking problem for hackney coaches. These plied for hire at cartstands in Westminster and shopkeepers complained that they blocked up the road when they were hanging about waiting for custom. There were traffic jams; a coach or carriage would overturn or run into something and cause mile-long queues. Pepys complains of the belligerent character of coachmen. In June 1663 he argued with a coach driver who wanted him to share the coach with another passenger and still pay full fare. By the reign of William III there were 700 hackney coaches in London.

There were other vehicles. Sedans were introduced in 1623 and there were a few in London throughout the century although they became really fashionable in the reign of Queen Anne.

Great families would have their own coach, which took them about town and into the country when they left their city house. In 1629 there were 500 coaches reported in London and Westminster.

Throughout London there were inns which the country coaches used as termini. The foot post, carrying letters, used to run between The Green Dragon in Bishopsgate and Bury St. Edmunds. The northern coaches came to the Belle Sauvage at Ludgate. By 1637 these regular routes were plying throughout the week. The carriers serving Brackley, Banbury and Buckingham did return journeys three times a week. By the end of the century fast coaches were travelling on main roads and changing horses en route. The great coaching days were to come but by the end of the 17th century Londoners were mobile. For the first time the ordinary citizen could travel outside his own backyard. He could write to friends too. Charles II patronised Dwbra's Flying Post, which delivered letters in the London area within 24 hours for twopence.

London Suburbs

London had been swallowing villages during the 17th century. Transport made them accessible. In the days of riding, a man had to be stalwart enough to walk or rich enough to ride, if he wanted to leave the city, but now carriers' wagons and coaches had diminished the miles. People who fled from the plague travelled as far as Wanstead; from the fire they travelled to Islington. These journeys were as long as a trip to Southend would be today. But little dormitories outside London did good trade in supplying the city. Market gardeners south of the river and dairy farmers in Hackney were prosperous enough for the areas to seem attractive and so the villages round London grew as well as the metropolis, and they were spreading, amoeba-like, towards the centre.

The 'service' areas round London were pitifully poor. St. Giles, which is the district round Oxford Street and the Tottenham Court Road junction, was filled with

The London Post, 1646. This service, 'communicating with the High Councils of both Parliaments of England, Scotland and other remarkable Passages both Civill and Martiall in his weekly travels through the three kingdoms', marked the beginning of a postal service.

dilapidated tenements jammed to capacity with porters, washerwomen, outdoor servants and labourers. When building workers came to London to gain employment after the Great Fire, they settled in districts like this, from which they could walk to their work without having to pay 'London' rents. The attraction in the Oxford Street area was the water supply. The great stone reservoir of London had been built there in the 13th century and its pipes still started from Stratford Place.

The Earl of Southampton had created a new estate in Bloomsbury, dividing his land into plots with a 24-foot frontage and letting them on long leases. Evelyn called the new area 'a little town'. It had its own centre,

Bloomsbury Square, and some of the buildings there and in Great Russell Street are altered relics of the 17th century new suburb.

Other suburbs had been created by the influx of foreigners, who peopled the less popular parts of London. The expansion east had been instituted by Huguenot refugees. Grounds which had been used for recreation were being encompassed, like Finsbury Fields and Moorfields. Chelsea would not be considered a satisfactory residential area until the 18th century—neither would Knightsbridge or Marylebone. If you lived in town you were still within easy walking distance of everything in the city. If you lived in the country you went right out of the area and came in by coach if necessary. Almost all the areas in London we know now were small communities consisting of a manor house, a few houses and a church; but they were in the country. There were miles of narrow lanes, heath and woodland between London and places like Hammersmith, Fulham, Dalston, Highbury and Paddington.

On the whole, the Londoners of 1688 could be very satisfied with their city; most of it was new. It seemed palatial compared with other European cities, which had not had the advantage of a great fire. It had first-class entertainment, an adequate water supply, indifferent sanitation, many open spaces and a cathedral under construction, which might be a wonder of the modern world.

The satisfaction had been expressed by one of the citizens, John Evelyn, thirty years before, who found 'London to be a town so nobly situated, and upon such a River, as Europe certainly shows not a more useful and agreeable'.

Places to Visit

The River

The Thames can be seen by walking along the Embankment from the Houses of Parliament to the Tower.

By underground: To Charing Cross, Northern, Bakerloo, Circle or District lines; or to Temple, Circle and District lines, closed on Sundays; or to Cannon Street and Blackfriars, Circle and District lines (Cannon Street, closed on Sundays); or to Tower Hill, Circle and District lines.

By bus (stopping on the Embankment): 109, 177, 184, 88, 159, 168, 77, 59, 3, 155.

The best way to see the river is by motor launch. You can travel by river to Greenwich; and from there visit the Queen's House, part of Greenwich Palace, built by Inigo Jones for Anne of Denmark; and see Christopher Wren's buildings (now the Royal Naval College) fronting the river. Services run from Westminster Pier and Charing Cross Pier to the Tower every 20 minutes from about 10.20 am. The charge is 4s. for the round trip. There are also trips to Battersea Park, Putney, Hammersmith, Kew, Richmond, Kingston and Hampton Court. Note: Advance information from Thames Launches Ltd., Thames Passenger Service, Westminster Pier, S.W.1. Tel. 930-2074.

The Suburbs

Moorgate, Finsbury Fields, Islington, Hampstead, Battersea, Bloomsbury and Chelsea can all be reached by public transport from the centre of London.

Museums to visit

British Museum

Address: Great Russell Street, W.C.1

Admission: Free

Opening hours: Monday—Saturday: 10 am—5 pm
                        Sunday: 2.30 pm—6 pm

Closed: Christmas Day and Good Friday
                        Open Bank Holidays usual hours

Access:

By Underground:

Tottenham Court Road (Central & Northern Lines)—turn right along Tottenham Court Road and right at Great Russell Street. Museum on left.

Russell Square (Piccadilly Line)—left out of station, cross Russell Square, and left on Montague Street to Great Russell Street and main entrance of Museum.

By Bus:

77, 68, 188, 196, to Southampton Row. Turn left along Great Russell Street.

73 to Tottenham Court Road/Oxford Street. Right along Great Russell Street.

7, 8, 23, 25, to Bloomsbury Way. Turn along Museum Street (from West).

7, 8, 22, 23, 25, from Holborn direction. Alight at High Holborn, just past Kingsway, and cross road, along Drury Lane or Grape Street, cross New Oxford Street and continue along Coptic Street or Museum Street.

By Car:

Drive from West along Oxford Street, turn left at Tottenham Court Road, and right almost immediately at Great Russell Street.

From East, along Holborn to Kingsway, turn right along

Southampton Row, and left at Great Russell Street.

N.B. There is limited parking at the Museum—otherwise, at side in Montague Street/Russell Square.

What to look for:
17th-century ceramics, glass, prints and drawings. Because of reorganisation of the museum, only a small selection is on view.

Guildhall Museum

Address :   On Bassishaw High Walk, up stairs by
                     Gillette House in Basinghall Street,
                     overlooking London Wall, E.C.2
Admission :   Free
Opening hours :   Monday—Saturday : 10 am—5 pm
Closed :   Sundays, Bank Holidays, Holy Days—
                     e.g. Christmas and Good Friday
Access :

By Underground:
Aldersgate (Metropolitan or Circle Lines)—turn right out of station along Aldersgate as far as London Wall. Turn left—Museum up on high walk-way opposite ruin of church tower.
St. Paul's (Central Line)—walk along Cheapside to Wood Street, left to Gresham Street, right for one block to Aldermanbury. Up stairs on right at end before junction with London Wall.
Moorgate (Metropolitan & Northern Lines)—turn right along Moorgate to London Wall. Turn right.
Bank (Central Line)—along Princes Street at side of Bank of England to Gresham Street. Left as far as Basinghall Street. Right. Museum at far end of Basinghall Street up steps by Gillette House.

By Bus:
7, 8, 22, 23, 25, to St. Paul's end of Cheapside, then follow instructions given under St. Paul's Underground
122

Station above.

76, 43, 21, 11, 9, 141, to London Wall/Moorgate. Follow instructions as from Moorgate Station.

By Car:

Parking is difficult except at weekends out of 'meter' hours. No parking at any time on London Wall.

From East: drive to the Bank then along Princes Street by Bank of England, turn left at Gresham Street, and right at Aldermanbury.

From West: Holborn/Newgate Street, turn left at Aldersgate and right at Gresham Street. Park in area behind Guildhall.

What to look for:

In the library are maps, topographical drawings, prints and reference books. On the stairs is the only known map of London by Ogleby and Morgan dated 1686.

London Museum

Address:	Kensington Palace
	Kensington Gardens, W.8
Admission:	Free
Opening hours:	March 1—September 30:
	10 am—6 pm (Sundays: 2 pm—6 pm)
	October 1—February 28:
	10 am—4 pm (Sundays: 2 pm—4 pm)
Closed:	Good Friday, Christmas Eve, and
	Christmas Day
Access:	

By Underground:

Queensway (Central Line)—cross Bayswater Road and walk through Broad Walk in Kensington Gardens to Palace.

Kensington High Street (Circle & District Line from Earl's Court to Edgware Road)—turn right along Kensington High Street to Park. Left through Park to Palace.

By Bus:
12, 88, along Bayswater Road to Queensway, then as above from Queensway Station.
9, 46, 52, 73, to Palace Gate in Kensington Road. Walk through Park to Palace.

By Car:
The best place to park is in the squares and side streets off Bayswater Road or Kensington Road. Then walk through Park.

What to look for:
The diorama on the fire, exhibits on the plague, the Cheapside Hoard, and other objects from Stuart London.

Victoria and Albert Museum

Address :   South Kensington, S.W.7
Admission :   Free
Opening hours :   Monday—Saturday : 10 am—6 pm
                    Sunday : 2.30 pm—6 pm
Closed :   Christmas Day and Good Friday
                    Open Bank Holidays usual hours
Access :

By Underground :
South Kensington (District, Circle and Piccadilly Lines)—a subway connects the station and the museum, giving entrance on N.W. (Exhibition Road) side. Main entrance to museum is on Cromwell Road.

By Bus:
207, 45, 49, to South Kensington Station.
14, 30, 74, to Brompton Oratory, at junction of Brompton Road and Cromwell Road.

What to look for:
Collection of panelled rooms (including one from Clifford's Inn), costumes, pottery and furniture. The Study Collections are closed on Sundays leaving only the Primary Collections on view.

124

Who's who in Stuart London

Buckingham, 1st Duke of (1592–1628): favourite of James I and Charles I. Built York House in the Strand and laid out area to Inigo Jones's watergate, still visible on the Embankment.

Buckingham, 2nd Duke of (1628–87): favourite of Charles II and a noted rake. Converted York House into speculative housing and rebuilt Wallingford House where Admiralty Arch now stands.

Charles I: Reigned 1625–49. Interested in fire precautions and Italianate architecture; instrumental in making Inigo Jones popular. Responsible for planning Whitehall Palace and allowed extension of Lincoln's Inn Fields and Great Queen Street. Executed in Whitehall.

Charles II: Restored to throne in 1660. Lived at Whitehall until death in 1685; encouraged the theatre and sport; made St. James's a fashionable centre; granted leases to extend St. James's.

Evelyn, John (1620–1706): A diarist, he noted London happenings during Commonwealth and reign of Charles II. Also a dilettante architect, submitted a plan for rebuilding London after the fire.

Gibbons, Grinling (1648–1720): A highly gifted woodcarver who also worked in stone and metal. In collaboration with Wren he decorated many City churches.

James I: Reigned 1603–25. Antagonised Londoners and his favourites were despised by the general public. Noted for his genuine learning and patronage of Inigo Jones. Believed in fireproof buildings and tried to reduce overcrowding.

James II: Reigned 1685–88. Dull, Catholic and tyrannical. Put down the Monmouth Rebellion with great severity, aided by Judge Jeffries.

Jones, Inigo (1573–1652): son of Welsh parents born in Smithfield, London. Travelled in Italy; combined with Ben Jonson in a series of court masques, but quarrelled with him repeatedly. Patronised by James I and Charles I, he rebuilt parts of London in the Italianate manner.

Milton, John (1608–74): lived in London most of his life, including a period at Whitehall as Cromwell's secretary with an office in Scotland Yard.

Pepys, Samuel (1633–1703): diarist and secretary to the navy in the time of Charles II. Gossiping, shrewd, and sociable, Pepys knew everyone and went everywhere. Christened in St. Bride's, Fleet Street; went to St. Paul's School; attended St. Olave's.

Rochester, Earl of (1647–88): profligate courtier of Charles II's reign; wrote plays and poems. Reputed to have disguised himself as a doctor and sold remedies to credulous Londoners in the streets.

Wren, Sir Christopher (1632–1723): Astronomer at Cambridge. Appointed assistant to Sir John Denham and submitted plan for new London in 1666, which was not used. His City churches are clustered around St. Paul's, his principal achievement.

Further reading list

Maurice Ashley   *England in the Seventeenth Century*, Penguin Books

F. R. Banks   *Guide to London*, Penguin Books

Daniel Defoe   *Journal of the Plague Year*

Isaac D'Israeli   *Curiosities of Literature*, George Parkledge (1866)

John Evelyn   *Diaries, Everyman Edition*, 2 volumes, J. M. Dent

Fuller   *Worthies of England*

Michael Harrison   *London Growing: The Development of a Metropolis*, Hutchinson

James Leasor   *The Plague and the Fire*, Pan Books

Malcolm Letts   *As Foreigners Saw Us*, Methuen (1935)

R. J. Mitchell and M. D. R. Leys   *A History of London Life*, Penguin Books

Thomas Platter   *Travels in England 1599*, translated by Clare Williams, Jonathan Cape, 1937

Steen Eiler Rasmusson   *London, the unique city*, Penguin Books

T. F. Reddaway   *The Rebuilding of London after The Great Fire*, Edward Arnold & Co., 1951

John Summerson   *Sir Christopher Wren*, 'Makers of History' series, Methuen

Gladys Scott Thomson   *Life in a Noble Household 1641–1700*, Jonathan Cape (1937)

Oliver Warner (Editor)   *Aubrey's Brief Lives*, Oxford University Press

Virginia Woolf   *Orlando*, Hogarth Press

Discovering London

Other Books in the Series

This volume is one of a set of eight books that trace the growth of London from Roman times to the end of Queen Victoria's reign. The other books are:

Set One

Set Two

Each title is available separately, price 6s. Alternatively each set of four volumes is available in a box with a fold-out map of the area, price 25s.